ENMITY BETWEEN

THE SEEDS

The End Revealed in the Beginning

Enmity Between

the Seeds

The End Revealed in the Beginning

Bill Cloud

Shoreshim Resources
Cleveland, TN

ENMITY BETWEEN THE SEEDS:
The End Revealed in the Beginning

ISBN 1-889931-36-5

First Printing - December 2004
Second Printing - October 2005

Unless otherwise indicated, Scripture quotations are from the New King James Version, © 1990, 1995 by Thomas Nelson Publishers, Nashville TN.

Cover design: Audra Mitchell, www.audramitchell.com
Cover artwork used by permission of artist:
Richard Kolseth, www.kolseth.net

Printed in the United States of America: Bayou Printing, Inc.

ACKNOWLEDGMENTS

Since this is my first solo work, at least as far as the printed page goes, it would be illogical to think that I did this all by myself. Nothing could be further from the truth! To begin with, Beth and the boys have devoted an incredible amount of time to leaving me alone to work. For Beth, this was quite a sacrifice seeing that in addition to her normal duties as matriarch of this household - attending a toddler and two teenagers, paying bills, etc. - she had to listen to me gripe when I could not write or when I dropped the computer that had the book stored on it (*that was a bad day*). She also corrected my spelling errors and grammatical shortcomings. Indeed, she deserves a blue ribbon for perseverance in the face of adversity.

Kudos to Keith and Paulette Johnson for providing a place of solitude during a crucial segment of the book and even more thanks to Paulette for her willingness to help with the editing process. Seeing that I write in much the same way that I speak, this was no easy undertaking.

Thanks also to Cindy Mason for transcribing a

recorded message, which proved to be the backbone of this book. Her efforts helped this project to actually get off the ground.

I also wish to give special thanks to Audra Mitchell for all of her help with our printed material, including but not limited to the cover design for this book. Her help has been priceless - literally! She did it all for no compensation.

I wish to commend my good friend Brad Scott of Wildbranch Ministry (www.wildbranch.org) for providing the missing piece of this puzzle. I can still remember the night two years ago when I walked into a tent and heard this guy teaching on the "Principle of the Seed." After he was done, I considered taking every teaching I had ever done, burning them and starting over. I didn't do that, but I did rethink a lot of what I had been taught. Furthermore, it became apparent, in dramatic fashion I might add, that the truth of this principle was the key to unraveling many end-time mysteries. For that reason, the seed principle is the bedrock of this project. Thanks to Brad for his friendship and for providing the Body with crucial information needed to understand the last days.

There are others who have, in some form or fashion, provided much needed support in this venture. Whether it was a simple word of encouragement or just a cup of black coffee, to all of you, I say thanks. I hope that when all who will read this work have finished the last page, they will be moved to say thank you as well. Each one of you contributed to the transformation of what started as a thought into a reality.

Bill Cloud
Cleveland TN, November 2004

CONTENTS

INTRODUCTION

"And I will put enmity between you and the woman, and between your seed and her seed; He will bruise your head and you shall bruise His heel." - Genesis 3:15

From the very moment he heard those words, I believe Satan has attempted to do to the righteous what was determined upon him, that is, bruise the head of the Promised Seed before his own head was bruised. Throughout the Scripture, we see this plan coming to the surface, but each instance resulting ultimately in failure.

Satan nevertheless, is not yet contained in a bottomless pit and, though defeated by the death, burial and resurrection of the Messiah, he continues to do his utmost to defeat the purposes of the God of Israel. The Scripture alerts us to this fact and, I believe, reveals to us, those he will be using in these last days in a final, futile attempt to crush those who would impede his designs, namely those who "keep the commandments of God and have the testimony of Jesus

Christ" (Rev. 12:17). To attract so much unwanted attention suggests that these particular followers of Messiah have become quite a threat to the kingdom of darkness. To be that great a threat further suggests that these people have matured spiritually beyond what can be observed presently in Christendom, at least as far as this writer is concerned.

For years, Christians have been clamoring for revival; an end-time revival unlike anything yet seen. That in itself acknowledges that something is either missing or needs restoring within the Body. Most of those who anticipate this last great spiritual renewal believe it will come just before the darkest days of human history - the Great Tribulation. It is believed that during this revival, unprecedented multitudes will respond to the Gospel as never before making this final harvest of souls the climactic event before the time to labor for the Kingdom of Heaven expires.

The truth is, there *will* be a final revival unparalleled in human history. There *will* be a great spiritual renewal and restoration in these last days. The prophet Amos referred to it as the revival of David's fallen tabernacle (Amos 9:11). The Apostle Peter referred to it as, "the times of restoration of all things" (Acts 3:21). Even the Messiah Himself acknowledged that before He returned there would be a time of revival and restoration, for He said, "Elijah truly shall come first and restore all things" (Mt. 17:11).

Yes, Scripture attests to this last day revival, and perhaps just as importantly, the faith and hope of many pines for and expects this restoration as well. In the past few years one of the more popular songs in the Body of Messiah has been *Days of Elijah*, a truly prophetic song that announces this season of revival.

This same longing has been expressed in synagogues for centuries through an ancient prayer:

"Bring us back LORD to you, and we shall return. Renew our days as of old."

As sincere as our desire for spiritual renewal may be, is it possible that what Scripture speaks of and what we have envisioned are two different things entirely? I suggest to you that, to a large degree, this is definitely the case. It is evident, I believe, by the fact that the end-time revival is already taking place and has been for some time now - right under our noses. Harvest time is already here!

Moreover, *because it is harvest time*, that means there are actually two revivals underway, each one unique in character and objective. How can we know this? Messiah revealed it to us through one of His most notable parables. The same parable also discloses that, unfortunately, these two revivals are not working in harmony, nor are they striving for the same goals. To the contrary, enmity exists between the two, and the unavoidable consequence is the climactic battle of an ages-old war.

The greater revival, the one born of God, will bring complete restoration to the earth and to God's people in fulfillment of His stated purposes. The promise of total redemption for those who place their trust in the LORD is as old as humanity itself, in fact older, for the Lamb was "slain, from the foundation of the world" (Rev. 13:8). Though His purposes and methods are at times concealed, they are nevertheless ultimately revealed to us through His Word. Therefore, as witnesses of prophecies fulfilled in the past and of those being fulfilled presently, this generation should discern that the time of our redemption draws near.

The latter and lesser revival, the one born of the Adversary, is a terrible resurgence of sacrilege and unprecedented murder, and is in response to the former. This revival, also predicted by Scripture, seeks to squelch or at least confound what God has intended not only for His righteous seed, but for Satan and his followers - that is, their complete and total destruction! Though his defeat is inevitable, still he tries, and has always tried, to undermine the plan of God for the sole purpose of survival and, perhaps, conquest. That, ladies and gentlemen, is precisely why the enemy of our soul continues with his efforts to strike a death blow to the righteous seed - he has no other choice.

To demonstrate this fact is the purpose of this book. My desire is to show the reader that the Adversary, from the very beginning, has pursued a plan that would, if successful, reverse the decision handed down to him in the Garden. His commitment to attaining this goal is the impetus of his existence, and so we see, the end of days *must* be characterized by a decisive battle between two seeds; one righteous, one wicked, one pro-Messiah, and the other anti-Messiah. One is God's seed while the other is the serpent's seed. The latter will employ weapons designed to spill blood. The former will overcome these weapons by the blood of the Lamb and by the word of their testimony (Rev. 12:11).

This is a comprehensive study of the battle between these two opposing seeds, how this ongoing struggle is being manifested in the world today and how, by the Holy Spirit, the Father is alerting His people of the impending danger. It is my prayer that when you have finished reading this book you will be convinced, as I am, that we are living in a time that, in Dickens' words is "the best of times and the worst of times." That the days are perilous there can be no doubt. We merely have to glance at the latest news reports to understand that. Yet, as has always been the case, the perils are indicators that the Adversary is attempting to prevent something glorious from happening. In other words, the unique dangers we presently face confirm that we are truly living in the days of restoration and redemption. So, do not be downcast about the future, but look up - your redemption draws near. These are days that have been revealed from the very beginning.

ONE

PRINCIPLE OF THE SEED

*"To you it has been given to know the mystery
of the kingdom of God." - Mark 4:11*

On the third day of Creation, Scripture declares
that the LORD God ordered the seas to gather together in one place so that dry land would appear. That
same day He commanded the earth to bring forth
seed.

*"Let the earth bring forth grass, the herb that yields
seed, and the fruit tree that yields fruit according to
its kind whose seed is in itself" - Genesis 1:12*

It is essential to our study to grasp two realities
revealed within the above passage of Scripture. The
first reality is: whatever the seed may be, that is what
the fruit will be. Whatever the fruit is, it is merely a
reflection of the seed within. Thus the statement,
"whose seed is in itself." This means that no one will

ever bite into an apple and find a peach pit in the core. The reason this will not happen is because God established the law that seeds should reproduce according to their own kind. If you observe anything that defies this law, then something is terribly wrong.

Interestingly enough, this law is the basis for the Messiah's counsel in how to deal with false prophets and false teachers. He admonished us to apply this principle when determining if their words are true or false.

> "You shall know them by their fruits. Do men gather grapes from thorns, or figs from thistles? Even so every good tree brings forth good fruit; but a corrupt tree brings forth evil fruit. A good tree cannot bring forth evil fruits, nor can a corrupt tree bring forth good fruit. . . . Therefore, by their fruits you shall know them." - Matthew 7:16-18, 20

The reason a corrupt tree cannot bring forth good fruit is because the seed that sprouted and grew into that corrupt tree was corrupt to begin with and may only reproduce after its own kind. Consequently, the fruit and the seed within are corrupt for the very same reason. In contrast to the corrupt tree is the good tree which produces fruit containing good seed simply because the original seed from which it grew was good. Therefore, we are to understand by Jesus' words that the principle of the seed is actually a spiritual concept revealed to us by the natural example. That brings us to the second reality revealed within Genesis 1:12.

Though this passage should be understood as referring to natural seed, it is important to understand

that the Word of God is not limited to natural dimen-
sions. We, who are mere humans, are three-dimensional beings living in a three-dimensional world, and
the LORD God transcends all that we comprehend.
Understanding this, are we then to believe that God's
Word, which is "living and powerful and sharper than
any two-edged sword" (Heb. 4:12), should be limited
to one dimension? I think not. Like God, His Word has
no beginning and has no end.

In other words, just as surely as God created
natural seed in the beginning, He established the seed
for spiritual things in the beginning, as well.
Furthermore, God has given us the natural things to
teach us of the more important spiritual matters. The
apostle Paul corroborates this truth in his epistle to the
Corinthians.

> *"There is a natural body, and there is a spiritual
> body. And so it is written, 'The first man Adam
> became a living being.' The last Adam became a life-
> giving spirit. However, the spiritual is not first, but
> the natural, and afterward the spiritual."*
> *- 1 Corinthians 15:44-46*

Put simply, natural things are given first in
order to teach us of the more substantial spiritual matters. For instance, God gave us the Primordial Light of
Creation in Genesis 1:3 to teach of the True Light of
Creation, the Messiah Jesus (hereafter to be referred to
as Y'shua). He gave us the weekly Sabbath to teach us
about the coming greater Sabbath when Messiah will
rule from Jerusalem, and the earth will enjoy a millen-
nial Sabbath rest.

Likewise, when He caused the earth to produce
seed on the third day of Creation, it was intended to

teach of the spiritual principle of the seed. The seed will produce fruit after its kind, and that fruit will contain the very seed that gave it life. In fact, the fruit exists because of and for the purpose of reproducing the seed, not the other way around. Unfortunately, as we have learned from Y'shua's words, not all seeds are good, and not all trees produce good fruit.

In the beginning there were two trees growing in the midst of the garden. One of them meant life, one of them resulted in death. These two trees and the fruit they bore, spawned by their respective seeds, were at enmity with one another. So from the beginning, there has existed a mutual antagonism between life and death, and between the righteous seed and the wicked seed. No amount of time, however long, will assuage that enmity nor negate the law that says each of these seeds must reproduce after its own kind. The righteous seed has always produced and continues to produce righteousness, even as the wicked seed continues to propagate its corruption. This is how it was in the beginning. This is how it will be in the end.

THE GOOD SEED

What is the good and righteous seed that produced the Tree of Life and the fruit that granted life eternal? A hint may be found in your local synagogue, for most Jewish houses of worship contain a wooden chest called the ארון הקודש *Aron Ha'kodesh*, or The Holy Ark. Within the ark behind a veil rests the ספר תורה *Sefer Torah*, or Torah scroll, that contains the Five Books of Moses, or more accurately, the Word of God!

Every Sabbath morning the *Sefer Torah* is removed from the ark, paraded through the midst of the congregation and then opened so that the words of God can be read for all to hear. When the *sefer torah* is returned to its resting place within the ark, the congregation stands and chants an ancient liturgical prayer.

> *Etz chayim hi, lama chazikimba,*
> *V'tomcheha m'ushar, d'racheha darche no'am*
> *V'chol n'tivoteha shalom, hashiveinu Adonai*
> *Elecha v'nashuva, chadesh, chadesh yameinu,*
> *Chadesh yameinu k'kedem*

The English interpretation of this prayer is:

> *"It is a tree of life to those who take hold of it,*
> *and those who support it are praiseworthy.*
> *Its ways are ways of pleasantness*
> *and all its paths are peace.*
> *Bring us back LORD to you, and we shall return.*
> *Renew our days as of old."*

What I wish for you to notice is that the "it" referred to in this prayer is the *sefer torah* - the Word of God - and is regarded as עץ חיים *etz chayim*, or "Tree of Life." It is Judaism's long-held belief that the "tree of life" in their synagogues is a representation of the Tree of Life that once adorned Eden. As a matter of fact, the panels on which the sacred words are written are referred to as "leaves," and the two spindles upon which the scroll is rolled are called the "branches."

So then, if tradition is to be trusted, this means that the Word of God is the Tree of Life which in turn produces the fruit of righteousness, and within that fruit resides the very seed that spawned it. That good seed is the Word of God (Lk. 8:11). When the LORD God caused the earth to produce seed that eventually sprouted and grew into fruit-bearing trees, it was His Word that caused this to happen. Should we then be surprised to learn that the most important seed - His Word - produced the most important tree, the Tree of Life? Every time Adam ate from this tree, the Good Seed - the Word - was implanted within Him. Had he not sinned, the Word of God would have sustained him for all time (Gen. 3:22).

THE PARABLE OF THE SOWER

Most everyone is familiar with the parable of the sower, and for that reason, I will not dissect it verse by verse. What I do wish to point out is that this parable is unique among all parables, because Y'shua tells us, if we are to understand all the other parables, then it is imperative to comprehend this one.

"And He said to them, 'Do you not understand this parable? How then will you understand all the parables? The sower sows the Word.' " - Mark 4:13, 14

This is fascinating when you think about it. If one can comprehend this parable, it will aid in unlocking any mystery contained within the others. Therefore, it behooves us to understand the principle of the seed. The seed is the focus of this parable, and according to Y'shua, the seed sown is the Word of God (Mk. 4:14, Mt. 13:19, Lk. 8:11). Furthermore, because the Messiah is the Word made flesh (Jn. 1:14), He is the seed *and* the One who sows the seed.

The Word is the Good Seed mentioned earlier, which was sown in the world at the very beginning of time. When this seed falls on good ground, it yields fruit, "some thirtyfold, some sixty and some a hundred" (Mark 4:8) and that means all this fruit contains the seed of the Word. Thus, this parable explains how the Word of God is scattered throughout the earth. It must first fall on good dirt - remember, we are made from the dust of the earth - and is further disseminated through those willing to receive the seed (the Word) with gladness and produce the fruit, which yields even more seed. There is a wrinkle in this process, however.

Occasionally the seed is scattered on the wayside and Satan (Gr. *satanas*) comes "immediately" to take away the Word that was sown in the hearts of those on the wayside. Considering that *satanas* means "adversary" and that this word, according to Thayer's definition, means "one who opposes another in purpose or act," is it possible that as he takes away the seed, he replaces it with something else - another seed perhaps - in an effort to effectively destroy the seed he opposes? Or, at the very least, is it possible that the Adversary would attempt to sow another aggressive seed in an attempt to restrain the Good Seed? Consider another well-known parable.

THE WHEAT AND THE TARES

"He put out another parable to them, saying, the kingdom of heaven is compared to a man who sowed good seed in his field, but while men slept, his enemy came and sowed tares among the wheat and went his way." - Matthew 13:24-25

We have all read this parable and have all heard opinions about its true message. Some consider it merely to be a description of the distinctions between "the Church" and "the World" and what happens to each party at the coming of the Son of Man. This is much too simplistic a view for such an important revelation. To truly grasp the entirety of what is being revealed to us, one must consider: a) the language of the message, b) the context of the message and c) the culture of those hearing the message when it was given.

As concerning the language of the message, let me clarify that Y'shua did not speak to this group in Greek. Some would say He spoke in Aramaic. Maybe, but for reasons I will not address in this publication, I tend to believe that He spoke in the language of the Scriptures, Hebrew. That being said, a few key words and phrases of this parable merit attention.

Even in Greek, the phrase "good seed" (*kalon sperma*) should be understood as speaking of seed which is morally pure, i.e. righteous seed. The Greek word *kalon* is used in the Septuagint (the Greek translation of the Hebrew Scriptures) primarily to convey an ethical concept, specifically, that which is first and foremost pleasing to the LORD. The Messiah verifies this ethical concept in Matthew 13:38 by interpreting the good seed as "the sons of the kingdom" which have been scattered by the Son of Man (Mt. 13:37).

One of the primary Hebrew words translated as *kalon* is the Hebrew טוב *tov*. In fact, the Hebrew equivalent of the phrase *kalon sperma* is זרע טוב *zera tov*. The word זרע *zera* is interpreted as "seed." The word טוב *tov* is "good" but not just in the sense of "as opposed to bad." *Tov* is a word that contains the sense of being singularly good, right and pure.

For instance, when in Matthew 19:17 Y'shua

said, "There is none good but one, that is, God," He would have used the Hebrew word *tov* to mean "good." Thus, there is only one "good," and it comes from God and is God. Likewise, there is only one Good Seed which comes from God, because He, the Word made flesh, is that Good Seed. The "sons of the kingdom" have that seed in them and are dispersed into the field, which is the world (Mt. 13:38), by the Son of Man - the Word (Mt. 13:37) - so that they may bring forth fruit. Yet, while men sleep, His enemy comes into the field to sow another seed (Mt. 13:25).

The word "enemy" in this case is *echthros* and is interpreted as one who is "actively hostile." *Thayer's Greek Definitions* says *echthros* is used to describe those "at enmity with God," and specifically refers to "the devil who is the most bitter enemy of the divine government." Y'shua confirms that this enemy is indeed Satan (Mt. 13:39), and the seed he scatters are his wicked children (Mt. 13:38). Think about this. If the sons of the kingdom are producing fruit that reflects the seed of the Word, then isn't it logical to assume that the "sons of the wicked one" will produce fruit that reflects the other seed within them?

A few years ago, I was sharing my views on this parable and its relevance to the end times with a group in Kentucky. After I had concluded my message an older gentleman approached me and introduced himself as a retired wheat farmer from Kansas. He told me that the parable of the wheat and tares held special meaning for him considering his background. He explained to me that when the two grow together, it is extremely difficult for the novice to notice the difference between the two, especially when they are young and immature.

He went on to explain that if one were to uproot the tares, or "cheat" (as he called it), he could not help but uproot the wheat as well, because the cheat tends to grow in the midst of the wheat. Not to worry though, at harvest it will be rather simple to distinguish between the two.

He related to me that, as the wheat grows and the fruit begins to appear on the heads of the wheat stalk, the maturing grain becomes heavy. The result is that, by the time of harvest, the weight of the mature fruit causes the wheat stalk to bow and, in a manner of speaking, humble itself before its Maker. The "cheat" or tare, on the other hand, has no weighty fruit to speak of and, consequently, does not bow but remains proud and erect. When harvest comes, those who reap have only to discern between the humble and the proud - the good fruit and the wicked fruit.

According to the Seed Principle, the good fruit - the wheat - are reflections of the seed that produced them. That the good seed in the parable matures into wheat should not be surprising considering that wheat is made into bread and bread is one of the basic necessities of life. The Messiah said that "Man shall not live by bread alone, but by every word that proceeds from the mouth of God" (Mt. 4:4). That Word, He said, was the true bread from Heaven, the "bread of life" and that He is that "bread which came down from Heaven" (Jn. 6:32-41). If He is the bread (the Word) and He is also the Seed (the Word), then it only makes sense that the Good Seed produces wheat, called here the "sons of the Kingdom."

According to the parable, the harvest comes at the "end of the age" (Mt. 13:38). The wheat is gathered into the barn (Mt. 13:30), but the tares are burned.

"Therefore as the tares are gathered and burned in the fire, so it will be at the end of this age. The Son of Man will send out His angels, and they will gather out of His kingdom all things that offend, and those who practice lawlessness, and will cast them into the furnace of fire. There will be wailing and gnashing of teeth." - Matthew 13:40-42

Biblically speaking, the tares, also called *darnel* in many translations, come from the Greek *zizanion*, which is actually believed to be a transliteration of the Hebrew זונים *zunim*. According to commentator David H. Stern, זונים *zunim* is a poisonous rye grass that looks like wheat until the heads appear. Other commentators note that, when ingested, *zunim* produce nausea, sleepiness, intoxication and even death. According to Judaism, *zunim* are essentially a degenerate form of wheat whose origins are traced to the time of the Flood.

"Rabbi 'Azaryah said in Rabbi Y'hudah's name, 'All acted corruptly in the generation of the Flood; the dog had intercourse with the wolf, and the fowl with the peacock; hence it is written, for all (flesh) on the earth had corrupted their way (Gen. 6:12).' Rabbi Julian ben Tiberius said in Rabbi Yitzchak's name, 'Even the earth debauched itself; wheat was sown and it produced zunim, for the zunim we find now came from the age of the Flood.' "
- Genesis Rabbah 28:8

Whether or not this is accurate is debatable, but it is, for reasons I will address later, extremely interesting. At any rate, the parable itself makes it clear that the *zunim* is the wrong kind of seed, and the fruit of that seed will be destroyed at the end of the age. Why? Because the wheat and the tare are distinguished by their respective natures - one good and one wicked. As a consequence, enmity exists between them. The degenerate seed will not be permitted to thrive when the Son of Man comes into His kingdom. It will be His seed, the Word, that will govern the nations.

> *"For out of Zion shall go forth the law (torah), and the Word of the LORD from Jerusalem. He shall judge between the nations." - Isaiah 2:3-4*

As a matter of fact, the Messiah states that, at the end of the age, "all things that offend and those who practice lawlessness" will be consumed. The word "offends" is to be understood as something that is both a "lure or trap" and "an impediment causing one to stumble." It is obviously implying something that causes one to sin against God's Word.

The word "lawlessness" is the Greek term *anomian*. The root of this term is *nomos*, or "law," and is the primary term used in the Septuagint to translate the Hebrew word *torah* (which actually means "instruction"). The point is, the Son of Man is going to remove those who are without Torah (those who practice lawlessness) and the degenerate seed that spawned them (all things that offend). Why? Because Torah, the Word of God, is the *only* seed that produces righteous fruit.

An important point to consider here is that when the Messiah first taught this parable as well as the parable of the Sower, there were no recorded Gospels, no Pauline epistles, no writings from Peter,

James or John. So, when He likened the Good Seed to the Word of God, what "Word of God" was He referring to? There can only be one answer - the Torah, or as most believers continue to refer to it, the Law of Moses. The writings of the prophets would also be considered the Word of God, but all of the prophets, without fail, continually encouraged the people of God to return to the Torah given to Moses. Messiah Himself warned those who opposed Him that their inability to believe Him was predicated on their failure to believe the writings of Moses (Jn. 5:39-47).

You see, whether it agrees with our theology or not, according to the Messiah, those without Torah have another seed; a corrupt seed that lures one into transgression of God's Word. As a matter of fact, the New Testament defines *sin* as "lawlessness" or *anomia* - "without Torah" (1 Jn. 3:4). The fruit this other seed produces is at enmity with the Word, because the Word, the Torah, is not in them. The tare is corrupt fruit - "By their fruits you shall know them" (Mt. 7:20). Therefore, it must be understood that there is only one Good Seed; anything else is corrupt. Moreover, good seed produces good fruit, while corrupt seed produces corrupt fruit. It can be no other way.

If it is true that there is only one Good Seed and every seed must yield fruit, "whose seed is in itself according to its kind" (Gen. 1:12), then that one Good Seed can *only* produce *one* Good Fruit. Any other fruit is of another seed. An apple seed does not produce a tree that bears apples, oranges, plums, etc. It produces one type of fruit - apples. Inside the apple is more apple seed. The reason for stressing this point is due to the fact that many believers presume that there are nine different fruits of the Spirit. However, Paul makes it clear that this perception is incorrect. There is but one good fruit.

> *"The **fruit** of the Spirit is love, joy, peace, longsuf-*
> *fering, kindness, goodness, faithfulness, gentleness,*
> *self control. Against such there is no law"*
> *- Galatians 5:22-23*

This is an extremely important point because if the principle of the seed is valid - one seed, one fruit - then it will be evident throughout Scripture. If it is a law that God has ordained, then it will never fail or change. Perhaps, this is one reason why the Messiah made sure to emphasize the Parable of the Sower and the mysteries contained therein - so that once we understood this principle, other mysteries would come to light.

In a private conversation the Messiah had with His disciples following the teaching of the wheat and tares, He clears up all the mysteries of the parable but one. He never really addresses "Why?" *Why* does the Adversary sow this wicked seed? We know there is hostility but why? Does he do it for spite, or is there a far more sinister plan at work? I believe the answer starts to come to light when we understand the context in which the parable was given.

According to Matthew 13, the wheat and tare parable is preceded immediately by the parable of the Sower - the one by which all other parables are understood. Based on what we learned, the Adversary obviously wants to contain, if not destroy, the Good Seed. Yet, if he can't completely destroy it, and if he can't contain it, perhaps his plan includes other objectives. I am suggesting that his intention is to profane the entire field - the world - by sowing bad seed. In this

way, according to God's own principles, he can poten-
tially undermine the plans and purposes of God.

At this point, I want to suggest to you that the
parable of the wheat and tares may very well be an
overview of human history as viewed from a spiritual
plane, for this parable reveals God's purposes and
those of His enemy. God, from the beginning, has
sought to spread the source of all that is good, the seed
of the Word, throughout humanity. The Adversary has
countered by sowing wicked seed in an effort to
defile, if not destroy, that which is good.

To grasp this view completely, the culture of
the day must be addressed, for it was Hebrew-speak-
ing, Torah-observant people to whom Y'shua spoke in
Matthew 13 and Mark 4. To the people of that culture,
elements of these parables, in particular the wheat and
tares, would have conveyed much more than what
they do to those of us immersed in western culture.

MINGLING THE SPECIES OF SEED

If one is to identify with the Israeli culture of
that day, he must acknowledge the role of the Torah in
everyday life. All the laws, statutes, ordinances and
commands were there, not only for cyclical purposes
(i.e. festivals and sabbaths), but also for day-to-day
living, including how and when one should sow and
reap his field.

Within the Torah there are specific laws known
as חקות *chukkot*, or laws seeming to have no obvious
reason for their inclusion in the Torah. Maimonides,
the famous Jewish sage (1136-1204 CE), observed in
regard to these types of laws that, "God has His reasons but no man can know them." Consequently,

these laws have been followed without raising too many questions. An example of these חקות *chukkot* is the negative law of forbidden mixtures known as כלאים *kil'ayim*, which means "mingled." According to the Torah, there are certain things that are mutually exclusive and should not be mixed together.

> *"You shall keep my statutes (chukkot). You shall not let your livestock breed with another kind. You shall not sow your field with mixed seed (kil'ayim). Nor shall a garment of mixed (kil'ayim) linen and wool come upon you." - Leviticus 19:19*

> *"You shall not sow your vineyard with different kinds of seed (kil'ayim), lest the yield of the seed which you have sown and the fruit of your vineyard be defiled." - Deuteronomy 22:9*

In both of these passages, the Torah forbids sowing with two different species of seed. In the second instance, the Scripture reveals that a field or vineyard sown with mixed seed will result in a defiled or corrupt crop to be consigned to the flames. So, we know why we should not mingle seeds - God has shown us the outcome - but we still don't understand *why* the mixed seed has this effect. Or do we?

First of all, we need to establish that, though rabbinic Judaism says we can't know the reason for this *chukkot* or statute, the truth is, we can. Once again, I will refer back to a principle the apostle Paul shared with the Corinthians; that God first gives the natural example (i.e. seed) so that we may learn of the greater spiritual concept (1 Cor. 15:44-46). As a matter of fact, Paul probably uses the laws prohibiting the mingling of seed as the basis for one of his directives to this same Corinthian congregation.

> *"Do not be unequally yoked together with unbelievers. For what fellowship has righteousness with lawlessness? And what communion has light with darkness? And what accord has Messiah with Belial? Or what part has a believer with an unbeliever? And what agreement has the temple of God with idols? For you are the temple of the living God. As God has said: 'I will dwell in them and walk among them. I will be their God and they shall be My people.' Therefore, 'Come out from among them and be separate says the LORD. Do not touch what is unclean, and I will receive you. I will be a Father to you and you shall be My sons and daughters, says the LORD Almighty.' " - 2 Corinthians 6:14-18*

If in the natural we are not supposed to mix the species of seed lest the outcome be defiled fruit, then it seems that when spiritual seeds - good seed and corrupt seed - are mingled together, the result is corrupt, unacceptable fruit, at least as far as a holy God is concerned. I suggest to you that this principle - not ethnic and cultural differences - is what Paul is referring to in the above Scripture.

The apostle argues that righteousness, which is the fruit produced by the seed of the Word, cannot fellowship with the corrupt fruit of lawlessness (*anomia*, "without Torah"). In essence, the Good Seed and the wicked seed are mutually hostile to the other, so why try to mix them? He also points out that because God is holy (Heb. קדוש *kadosh*, "set apart") and because He dwells in us, by His nature, He cannot co-exist with corrupt seed. Thus, He calls us to be "set apart' and to retain our purity as Good Seed, unfettered from the restraints of corruption and wickedness.

From the Adversary's point of view, restraining the progress of the righteous seed is exactly what he had and still has in mind. In fact, I was rather fascinated to discover that the root word of כלאים *kil'ayim*, "mingled," is the Hebrew word כלא *kala*, which means "to restrict or hold back." It is also the root of the Hebrew word for "prison." The implications are very clear; sowing with mingled seed impedes and undermines the *purpose* of the seed, both naturally and spiritually. To cavort and mingle with unrighteousness simply places God's people in bondage to the designs of the enemy and the works of the flesh.

In Deuteronomy 22:9, the Torah says that sowing with mingled seed defiles both "the yield of the seed" and "the fruit of your vineyard." Though these two phrases suggest similar meanings in English, in Hebrew there seems to be a slight distinction between them. The "yield" is the Hebrew מלאה *m'leah* and means "something fulfilled." It comes from another word, מלא *ma'le*, which means "fullness, accomplished, to come to an end." In other words, "the yield" refers to what the seed accomplishes, its fullness, or shall I say, the purpose of the seed, whereas "the fruit of your vineyard" is referring to the actual crop of fruit.

Again, the Torah teaches that sowing with mingled seed not only defiles the fruit, which is now contaminated, but also undermines the purpose of the seed. As I have stated previously, this has been Satan's objective from the beginning. No wonder he is portrayed as the enemy (Gr. *diabolos*, "slanderer, false accuser") who comes into another's field sowing degenerate seed. This is what I believe Y'shua was conveying to His listeners, if they had "ears to hear." They certainly should have understood the significance of someone sowing another species of seed in a field sown with wheat. Due to their Torah-based culture, this action would have been viewed as a deliberate attempt by a malicious individual to defile the purpose of the man's seed and to ruin his crop.

If they had understood the parable of the sower, the significance of the seed, and what the Adversary attempts to do in opposition to the Word, they could have seen the parable of the wheat and tares for what it is - a vivid description of the ongoing conflict between the purposes of God and the designs of the Adversary. The purpose of God is, of course, to spread the seed of the Word throughout the world until all is fulfilled.

The strategy of the Adversary is to use all means at his disposal to resist the spread of the Word - snares, lies, intimidation, etc. Because Y'shua refers to him as "the devil" (Mt. 13:39), which is *diabolos* - "a slanderer" or "false accuser" - there is reason to believe that he uses his mouth, *his word*, in this quest to restrain the Word of Truth. It should also be noted that, from the beginning, the serpent's word has always contained a measure of truth *mingled* with lies. This point will come to bear later in the book.

To the world's misfortune, the parable suggests that the Adversary has been marginally successful, yet, I wish to point out that it was the owner of the field who permitted the two seeds to grow along side one another, knowing that as they matured, the differences between the good and bad would become obvious. He knew that at harvest - the end of the age - the laborers would have no trouble distinguishing between the two and rectifying this unfortunate dilemma.

So, by understanding key principles within the Torah and through the revelation provided to us by the Messiah, specifically in Mark 4 and Matthew 13, we can see how God intended things to be in the beginning and how the Adversary sought to corrupt those intentions. That in turn helps us to better understand how things will be in the end. Frankly, the parable of the wheat and tares is, perhaps, more important for this generation to understand than it was for the generation who were there to hear the Messiah personally. We are truly living in the time of the harvest, and just as the parable foretold, there are two seeds growing along side each other to this day. Because of their opposing natures inherent within the seed that spawned them, there exists a mutual uneasiness with the other, a simmering hostility between them - enmity. Who can say what may happen just before they are separated from one another? Yet before I address that question, it is important to first acknowledge another mystery of the kingdom.

$\mathcal{T}$wo

THINGS CONCEALED, THINGS REVEALED

"Nothing is hidden which will not be revealed, nor has anything been kept secret but that it should come to light." - Mark 4:22

At this juncture, I feel it is important to briefly summarize what we have learned so far about the seed, because these points are fundamental if we are to grasp what the Father is trying to show His people about the end of days.

* *The seed for everything is in the beginning.*
* *Seed reproduces after its kind.*
* *There is only one good seed, the Word of God.*
* *There is enmity between good and wicked seed.*
* *God forbids the mingling of seeds.*

Now, imagine the Good Seed lying in a freshly plowed field. Just like other seeds, it lies in the ground waiting for the right conditions that will allow it to germinate beneath the surface and set down its roots just before it breaks through the surface of the soil.

When it does, what once was concealed will be revealed. That which was hiding beneath the surface is now out in the open and, being nurtured by the sun, begins to grow and flourish. When all has performed its purpose, the harvest will see the fruits of that seed gathered in. Y'shua expounded on this process.

> *"The kingdom of God is as if a man should scatter seed on the ground, and should sleep by night and rise by day, and the seed should sprout and grow, he himself does not know how. For the earth yields crops by itself; first the blade, then the head, after that the full grain in the head. But when the grain ripens, immediately he puts in the sickle, because the harvest has come." - Mark 4:26-29*

According to the Messiah, the very reason the seed goes through this process is to produce a harvest of fruit which is, in essence, an innumerable reproduction of the original seed. God sowed the Good Seed in order to produce an immense harvest of fruit "whose seed is in itself." When the fullness of that harvest comes, the reaping will begin suddenly.

Before the harvest comes though, the seed must germinate. Once it does, one of the first things the seed will do is put down roots. Of course, the roots continue to grow beneath the surface because they serve as the heart and anchor of the plant, or for the sake of our illustration, the tree. Acting as the heart, the root system pumps all the nutrients the tree will need to thrive and produce fruit.

As the anchor, the roots aid in the stability, and consequently, the longevity of the tree. So then, we are faced with the fact that, it is not the branches, foliage or trunk of the tree that is most important, but the concealed roots born of a tiny seed. This is not to say that the other components are unimportant, for they too came from the same seed. Furthermore, the part above the surface is where the fruit will grow.

Nevertheless, trees will lose their foliage and live. At times, branches are broken off and the tree lives. Even the trunk can be damaged by a lightning bolt and survive, but when that part of the tree concealed beneath the surface is severely damaged, slowly but surely, the tree withers and dies.

This natural reality leads to this conclusion: what we do not see oftentimes upholds what we do see. Those things concealed are most likely the foundation for things which are revealed. Even though, contextually, Paul was referring to another issue, he nevertheless points out in Romans 11 that, "You (the branches) do not support the root, but the root supports you" (Rom. 11:18).

THE HIDDEN FOUNDATION

How many times have you or someone you know walked into a room, surveyed the walls, ceiling and fixtures and remarked, "Wow! This building surely has a great foundation." Chances are, not very many, if at all. However, we are all aware that each sound structure we see has a foundation concealed beneath all that we can observe. The reason for confidence in a foundation we cannot see is because of the stability of what we can see - the walls, the ceiling, etc. What I can see tells me there is a foundation beneath me, demonstrating once again that things natural can teach us of a greater spiritual principle.

The notion that things concealed are the foundation for things revealed has been investigated, to say the least, by rabbis throughout the centuries. Their perspective of this is found within an ancient concept referred to as פרדס *pardes*, meaning "garden" or "orchard," interestingly enough. This methodology analyzes the Scriptures, and specifically the Torah, using four basic categories of interpretation. These four categories are recognized as having equal validity in their own area, since according to rabbinic tradition the Bible is like a rock which can be split into many pieces under the hammer of interpretation. The four categories are listed here. (Notice the first letters of each word form the acronym P-R-D-S or *pardes*.)

* פשת *Peshat* - *The simple or literal meaning.*
* רמז *Remez* - *The meaning hinted at in Scripture.*
* דרוש *Derush* - *The homiletic meaning of the text.*
* סוד *Sod* - *The secret or concealed meaning.*

The first category, the literal application, is self-explanatory, so I will not devote any space to explaining it further. However, for the sake of clarity, I want to briefly expound upon the second and third categories before moving on to the all-important fourth category, the focus of our study.

An example of רמז *remez*, or "hint" could be found in many Scriptures, but I will use just one illustration of this concept.

"The angel of the LORD encamps all around those who fear Him, and delivers them." - Psalm 34:7

Literally, we are told that those who fear the LORD have the promise of angelic protection. It is this literal statement that actually *hints* at the other obvious conclusion, which is, those who do not fear the LORD have no such promise. Therefore, the Scripture teaches, though in this instance it does not explicitly state it, that those who go about their lives showing no fear of God do so at their own peril. This is an example of Biblical interpretation using *remez*.

Derush דרוש, the category assigned for the homiletic meaning, is a word whose root, דרש *darash*, actually means, "to seek, investigate, to demand." It is understood that what is being demanded is an interpretation, an explanation. For those who have heard of the מדרש *Midrash*, a collection of biblical interpretations collected from the Oral Torah, you should recognize the similarity in these two words; מדרש *midrash* and דרוש *derush* are derived from the same root word.

Derush, then, seeks to find answers to Biblical questions by applying the biblical adage, "Precept upon precept..., line upon line, here a little, and there a little" (Isa. 28:10). In other words, one must not concoct a doctrine or belief based on one Scripture, and especially if it is taken out of context. Sound doctrinal interpretation is based on a concert of Scripture. Many times we find that the various elements of interpretation are brought together by allusions made within the Scripture. The Apostle Paul called upon this authentic and Hebraic method of interpretation many times while addressing issues within the Body.

"Why do you judge your brother? Or why do you show contempt for your brother? For we shall all stand before the judgment seat of Messiah. For it is written: 'As I live, says the LORD, every knee shall bow to Me, and every tongue shall confess to God.'"
- Romans 14:10-11

Nowhere are we told in the passage Paul quoted (Isa. 45:23) that we are not to judge our brother, yet Paul arrives at that conclusion and makes an authoritative statement. What in Isaiah's passage gives him that authority? Isaiah declares that all will be humbled before the Supreme Judge. Paul can rightfully conclude that because every knee shall bow, no one has the right to show contempt for or pass judgment on his brother. This is a very basic example of biblical interpretation using the methodology of *derush*.

I might point out also, that Y'shua taught in this manner as well. As He was dying upon the tree, He exclaimed, *"Eli, Eli, lama shabachthani,"* which is, "My God, my God, why have you forsaken me?" (Mt. 27:46). Why did He say this? Was it because the Father had turned His back on the Son? Probably not. It is more likely that Y'shua was simply alluding to Psalm 22, which begins with *"Eli, Eli, lama shabachthani."* As you continue to read the Psalm it becomes apparent that Y'shua was not mourning the Father's rejection, but was simply trying to point out to those witnessing His execution that He was the one David had written of centuries before.

Now we come to the fourth and perhaps the most intriguing of these categories of interpretation - סוד *sod*, (pronounced *sode*) or "secret." I should point out first of all that by "secret" I do not mean to say "occultic." This is not in any way related to the mystery religions or secret societies and their mystic rites. *Sod* or "secret" is to be understood as being "concealed" in the same way a foundation is concealed from view, and still we know it is there. The hidden "foundation" is the principal reason things revealed are sustained.

Rather than show examples of this concept here, I intend to demonstrate this particular principle at length in the ensuing chapters. Instead, here I would like to bolster the notion that it is things concealed that actually serve as the foundation for things revealed. The method I wish to employ at this point is the Hebrew language itself.

Sod, "secret," is spelled ס samekh, ו vav, ד dalet. By placing the smallest Hebrew letter, called י yod, at the beginning of the word סוד sod, the result is the word יסוד yesod. This result is very interesting for yesod is the Hebrew word for "foundation."

סוד   יסוד

Sod - "secret"   Yesod - "foundation"

So, is the actual language of the Bible testifying that things hidden are actually upholding those things that we can perceive? I am certainly not trying to negate or diminish the crucial importance of the simple and literal meaning, but as I have noted before, the natural revelations often, if not always, render the service of pointing us to the greater spiritual principles.

It is at least possible that, on many occasions, what the Word reveals to us on the surface of the text may be there to teach us about what is beneath the surface of the text - the foundation. It is crucial to remember that God is without dimension. He cannot be contained by our sense of logic. His thoughts are above our thoughts. Accordingly, the Bible teaches us that He conceals messages within the text of Scripture.

The Hidden Dimension of the Torah

Most believers have never heard of the "inner dimension of the Torah," yet for those astute in Judaism, this is a very well-known theme. So well-known, in fact, that the unveiling of this "inner dimension" is considered to be one of the greater signs of the Messiah's arrival. According to one treatise on the subject, "Messiah would reveal altogether new insights, making manifest the hidden mysteries of the Torah." Rabbinic commentary has something to add as well.

> *"All the Torah learned in the present world will be vain compared to the Torah of Mashiach."*
> *- Kohelet Rabba 11:12*

If this belief is such an integral part of Judaism's expectations of the Messiah and his role in the future, certain questions must be asked. To begin with, why hasn't mainstream Christianity addressed this issue? Secondly, where did this idea come from - tradition or Scripture? In response to the first question, the attitude of Christendom at large is; "Since the Torah is not for us but for the Jews," the point is moot. Unfortunately, this errant stance has robbed us of a treasure-trove of information, an example of which we will be sharing in subsequent chapters.

Both tradition and Scripture is most likely the proper reply to the second query. Yet in the case of tradition, it has more to do with the traditional methods of dissecting the Word of God (i.e. *pardes*) as opposed to some fanciful legend. You see, understanding that the Scripture teaches on multiple levels is nothing new, but is indeed an ancient traditional belief. It is the nuances of the Hebrew language itself that leads one to this conclusion. For instance:

"It is the glory of God to conceal a matter; but the glory of kings is to search out a matter."

- Proverbs 25:2

Even on the surface, the English text indicates that God does conceal things, and that these matters can be unearthed. The English does not disclose, however, *what* things are being concealed and revealed. Where are these unidentified "matters" hidden, and where do we look in order to find them? With all due respect to the English translators and commentators, if we limit our Biblical knowledge to their scriptural fluency, some answers will never materialize. On the other hand, if we expand our quest for knowledge to include study of the Hebrew text using time-tested Hebraic methods of study, the smoke begins to clear.

In the Scripture above, the Hebrew word that is translated as "matter" is דבר *d'var* which, according to *Brown-Driver-Briggs' Hebrew Definitions*, is "a matter, a word, saying or utterance." In other words, it is to God's glory to conceal "a matter" but that matter may actually be "a word or saying" that we need in order to flourish spiritually. It is to our benefit to dig deep below the surface of the text, to investigate and thoroughly examine this concealed "word" and then, through *midrash*, comprehend the ramifications. In essence, God conceals Himself so that we will be provoked to look for Him.

This is what rabbinic scholars have done for centuries, and as a result, many details concerning the Scriptures that would have otherwise remained secret have been made known. Yet, in their search of the Scriptures, they were forced to acknowledge that there remained many utterances whose true meaning had not yet seen the light of day. They became convinced that there was indeed a hidden, "inner dimension" of the Torah, which could only be revealed by the "anointed one," the Messiah.

> "Give ear, O my people, to my law (torah). Incline your ears to the words of my mouth. I will open my mouth in a parable; I will utter dark sayings of old, which we have heard and known, and our fathers have told us. We will not hide them from their children, telling to the generation to come the praises of the LORD." - Psalm 78:2

Not only did Y'shua confirm the belief in an "inner dimension" of the Torah, but actually began to reveal this inner dimension in just the way the Psalmist said He would.

> "All these things Y'shua spoke to the multitude in parables; and without a parable He did not speak to them, that it might be fulfilled which was spoken by the prophet, saying: 'I will open my mouth in parables; I will utter things kept secret from the foundation of the world.' " - Matthew 13:34-35

He confirmed to His disciples that there were mysteries of the kingdom and these mysteries were being revealed to them by Him.

> "And the disciples came and said to Him, 'Why do you speak to them in parables?' He answered and

44

said to them, 'Because it has been given to you to know the mysteries of the kingdom of heaven, but to them it has not been given.' " - Matthew 13:10-11

In this excerpt from Matthew 13, the word "mysteries" merits special consideration. The Greek word translated here is *musterion* and means "something concealed." According to the commentator Albert Barnes (1798-1870 CE), "It does not mean that the thing was incomprehensible or even difficult to understand . . . it simply means it had not been before made known." Thayer defines it as "a hidden or secret thing, not obvious to the understanding." He also adds that, "In rabbinic writings, it denotes the mystic or hidden sense of an Old Testament saying."

It seems obvious to me, considering what we have learned about Judaism's recognition of this hidden wisdom, that Y'shua was a) meeting their Messianic expectations concerning this issue and b) confirming that there is such a thing as a concealed "inner dimension" of the Word of God. The Father has and presumably does conceal principles within His Word.

PAUL AND THE HIDDEN WISDOM

For more corroboration of this reality, let us now look to the apostle Paul. Keep in mind that Rav Shaul, as he would have been known, was trained in Torah at the feet of Rabban Gamaliel the Elder (Acts 22:3). There are some who have theorized that, owing to both his talent and prestigious credentials, Paul may have been in line to preside over the *Sanhedrin*. At the very least, we know that he was present from time to time when the *Sanhedrin* convened. We certainly know that he was in attendance on the occasion of Stephen's trial (Acts 7:58; 22:20). The point is that Paul was well trained in the principles of Torah study.

Therefore, he would be well acquainted with the rationale associated with the four levels of Torah study - *peshat, remez, derush* and *sod*. So then, his acknowledgment of a God-ordained "hidden wisdom" should come as no surprise now that we are aware of what this hidden wisdom is.

> *"We speak wisdom among those who are mature, yet not the wisdom of this age, nor of the rulers of this age, who are coming to nothing. But we speak the wisdom of God in a mystery, the hidden wisdom which God ordained before the ages for our glory, which none of the rulers of this age knew; for had they known they would not have crucified the Lord of glory. But as it is written: 'Eye has not seen, nor ear heard, nor have entered into the heart of man the things which God has prepared for those who love Him.' But God has revealed them to us through His Spirit. For the Spirit searches all things, yes, the deep things of God." - 1 Corinthians 2:6-10*

These are the words of a Torah scholar intimately familiar with the Hebrew language and initiated in the ancient traditions of Scriptural interpretation. So, when he refers to hidden wisdom that God foreordained, he can only be speaking of one thing - the "inner dimension" of Torah and those things regarded as *sod* or "mysteries."

The phrase "hidden wisdom" is translated from the Greek *apokrupto*, which means "to hide or conceal." (*Krupto* is the origin of our word *cryptic*). *Apokrupto* is the same word used in the *Septuagint* to translate "conceal" in Proverbs 25:2 - "It is the glory of God to *conceal* a matter..." Paul says these concealed matters were ordained of God before time "for our glory." The Greek *doxa*, "glory," is also used in the *Septuagint*'s translation of Proverbs 25:2 - "It is the *glory* of kings to search out a matter." Is it possible that Paul is thinking of this ancient Proverb and the concept of "hidden wisdom" it hints of as he writes his letter to the Corinthians?

The particular mystery that Paul addresses in 1 Corinthians 2 just happens to be the mystery of mysteries as far as Torah is concerned - the death and resurrection of the Messiah. Paul makes it clear that this mystery was so deeply concealed that the princes of this world had been unable to discern God's plan. Furthermore, it seems obvious that God's overall plan included their lack of detection for, as Paul notes, had they unraveled this mystery of mysteries they would have never allowed the Messiah to be crucified. Without the crucifixion, there is no resurrection and we would still be in our sin. (1 Cor. 15:17)

If referring to earthly princes, i.e. the Jewish rulers, teachers and scribes of the day, it is logical to assume they would not have killed the One they were seeking had they recognized Him. On the other hand, Y'shua had gone to great lengths to prove He was the One and still they could not, or would not, acknowledge Him (see Mt. 16:1-4). It bears noting that these rulers were the very ones who supported the ancient notion that Messiah would reveal things hidden from the foundation of the world.

If Paul refers to spiritual princes, the rulers of

the darkness of this world, they would certainly not consciously follow through with an agenda that led to their own destruction. In other words, had they understood what the Messiah was to accomplish and how, they would have kept Him alive. Obviously, these principalities had not discerned that the Messiah was to die and to rise again, yet the revelation and doctrine of the Messiah and all that it entails has always existed within the words of the Torah.

"Then I said, 'Behold I come; in the scroll of the book it is written of me.' " - Psalm 40:7

"The Lamb slain from the foundation of the world." - Revelation 13:8

Let us go one step further with this. It is very apparent that, not only did the rulers of this world fail to see the plan of God as it relates to the Messiah, but the Messiah's own followers were slow to see what the Torah had already ordained. Consider the conversation between Y'shua and two of His disciples on the way to Emmaus.

To begin with, these two men could not see it was the Messiah they were conversing with. To this "stranger" they expressed regret that the One they supposed to have been the Redeemer of Israel had been put to death, yet, puzzlement at the news of His resurrection. Y'shua's reply came quickly.

" 'O foolish ones, and slow of heart to believe in all that the prophets have spoken! Ought not the Messiah to have suffered these things and to enter into His glory?' And beginning at Moses and all the

prophets, He expounded to them in all the Scriptures the things concerning Himself."
                                            - Luke 24:25-27

These were men who knew Him and believed in Him, and still they had not seen beforehand "these things" Messiah was to suffer before entering His glory. Where were these things to be found? Y'shua points to Moses (Torah) and the prophets. But before we castigate them for their faux pas, recall that in Matthew 13:11, Y'shua Himself refers to the "mysteries of the kingdom" which were being revealed to some and not to others. These "mysteries" were truths purposely kept secret from the beginning of time but at His coming were being revealed to those who had ears to hear. And how are these truths revealed? According to Paul, the understanding of this hidden wisdom comes not from rabbinic sages or televangelists but by the Holy Spirit.

"But God has revealed them to us through His Spirit. For the Spirit searches all things, yes, the deep things of God." - 1 Corinthians 2:10

When Y'shua asked His disciples, "Who do you say that I am?" (Mt. 16:15), Peter's confession that He was the Messiah and Son of the Living God prompted the Messiah to exclaim:

"Blessed are you, Simon Bar-Jonah, for flesh and blood has not revealed this to you, but My Father who is in heaven." - Matthew 16:17

In other words, the ever-present truth concerning the Messiah's true nature and identity was nevertheless concealed from the very foundation of the world. But when it was time for this truth to be disclosed, the One who had ordained that it should be hidden is the same One who revealed it to Peter. This secret - this *sod* - is the very foundation (*yesod*) of our faith, for Messiah states:

> *"And I also say to you that you are Peter, and on this rock I will build My congregation, and the gates of Hades shall not prevail against it." - Matt. 16:18*

This truth - that Y'shua is the Messiah and Son of God - is the rock upon which we stand. It is the basis for all that is true and the very cornerstone of the Kingdom. It is the same hidden truth Paul speaks of when He declares the gospel of Y'shua the Messiah "and him crucified" (1 Cor. 2:2). Thus, once again, we see that things concealed are the foundation for things revealed. Still, seeds do eventually germinate and break out of subterranean darkness and into the light.

Nothing Before Its Time

In natural terms, a seed lies beneath the surface of the ground, concealed from view, and will not sprout and bring forth the blade UNTIL it is time. Soil conditions, moisture, temperature and all the necessary ingredients for that seed to grow work in harmony with the proper season. But when it is time, the seed sprouts and grows quickly, ultimately bringing forth the fruit the sower knew was contained within the seed when he planted it.

From our perspective as believers two thousand years after the fact, it is easy to see the Messiah's death, burial and resurrection throughout the text of the Torah. Yet at that time, most people did not see this aspect of the Messianic prophecies. It was like that seed hidden beneath the ground known only to the One who sowed it. Without question, certain aspects of the Messianic Promise were not understood because they were concealed *until* it was time for them to be revealed. When it was time, events unfolded quickly. As it is written:

> *"But when the fullness of the time had come, God sent forth His Son." - Galatians 4:3*

So, as we have seen with the Messiah, some truths that have always been present within the Word lie dormant beneath the surface of understanding and spring to life *only* in the proper season. Some things simply can't be understood until it is the right time, thus the prophet records:

> *"Write the vision and make it plain on tablets, that he may run who reads it. For the vision is yet for an appointed time; but at the end it will speak, and it will not lie. Though it tarries, wait for it; because it will surely come, it will not tarry."*
> *- Habakkuk 2:2-3*

In the beginning, the Father of the world planted many seeds, not all of them natural. He knows what is going to happen today, tomorrow and into eternity, because He is the One who planted the origin of future events. He knows of every hidden truth lying beneath the surface waiting only for the proper season before bursting into the light of comprehension.

Hence it is possible, if not probable, that there are other crucial and eternal truths that we have yet to ascertain. Do we really believe that we have learned all there is to learn about the Word? According to Paul, the answer is a resounding "No." Again speaking of these hidden truths, he says that:

> *"Eye has not seen, nor ear heard, nor have entered into the heart of man the things which God has prepared for those who love Him."* - 1 Corinthians 2:9

Contrary to popular belief, this passage of Scripture is not speaking of heaven. It is not speaking of the hereafter but addresses the fact that there are secrets yet to be uncovered. Considering the context of Paul's statement, it must be concluded that these hibernating kernels of truth are concealed beneath the surface of sacred Scripture, specifically the Torah. Note what the Messiah says about this subject.

> *"Therefore every scribe instructed concerning the kingdom of heaven is like a householder who brings out of his treasure things new and old."*
> - Matthew 13:52

Scripture, like its Author, is fathomless, so who among us can say that they understand all mysteries? No, it has not yet occurred to us all that God has deposited within His Word and especially those things pertaining to the end of days. No one has fully considered or understood all the hidden truths destined to affect the entire world. Only the One who planted the seed of future events can say:

"I am God, and there is none like Me, declaring the end from the beginning." - Isaiah 46:9-10

However, if we are instructed concerning the Kingdom of Heaven, if we understand the parable that unlocks all other parables - the Seed and the Sower - then we are equipped to uncover "treasures new and old" provided that we are prepared to fine tune some aspects of our theology.

It should be noted that many of the scribes and spiritual leaders of the Messiah's day felt fairly confident about their interpretation of Scripture, including those passages alluding to the Messiah and the end of the age. Presumably, it was this confidence that convinced them to label the true Messiah a blasphemer. In part, it was their theology that blinded them to the fact that prophecy was being fulfilled even as they were longing for its fulfillment.

Perhaps the same could be said of our day. When it comes to eschatology, theologians as well as laymen have pretty much decided how the end time will unfold. Sure, there are certain elements that remain a mystery, but for the most part, a basic scenario remains entrenched in our dogma. As I see it, the fundamental flaw in our prophetic dogma is that, for the most part, we tend to interpret the end from the end in spite of the fact that God declares the end from the beginning! That beginning, and consequently sound doctrine, is written in the Torah.

It is my strong conviction that certain prophetic truths, long concealed, are now being revealed simply because it is time. Some of these truths will challenge long-held beliefs and therefore require that we judge them according to the Scripture and not according to our philosophy or even, in some cases, our theology. To truly comprehend the end, we must return to and decipher the beginning. It is there in the genesis of history that we will find the seeds for these revelations, if we know how to look for them. That is, in fact, the purpose for these first two chapters; to establish key principles that will aid us in this search.

As we look at the beginning we will be able, through the Hebrew language and ancient methods of study, to uncover the סוד *sod* or "secret" lying beneath the surface of the text. It is there that we will search for the word - דבר *d'var* - the Father has concealed (Prov. 25:2) concerning the end of days. It is indeed to our benefit to find and understand the ramifications of this hidden wisdom, so, let us go to the beginning so that we may correctly interpret the end.

Three

In The Beginning

"Now the serpent was more cunning than any beast of the field which the LORD God had made." - Genesis 3:1

On occasion I am sure that most of us have read the Scriptures in a casual manner, never really engaging the meaning of the text we are reading at the time. Be aware! This can become habit forming and the results unfavorable to our mission as believers. By consistently using this approach to the Bible, we tend to arrive at superficial conclusions about the text, or worse, we rely on others - scholars for instance - to properly interpret the Scripture for us.

The problem with the latter is, apparently, this same debility affects "scholars" as well. Throughout history, scholars have been found to be fallible in one point or another. Scholars have not resolved all mysteries, and often "their" conclusions were taught to them by someone else who arrived at superficial conclusions because they didn't take the Bible literally.

It was told to me by a friend that a very well-known prophecy teacher once admitted that, on the occasions he had ignorantly misrepresented the meaning of Scripture, it was almost always due to not interpreting the Bible as literally as he should. We are all guilty at times of this egregious error. We allegorize a passage meant to be taken literally or perhaps consider its words to be nothing more than poetic pageantry. What would happen, though, if we started looking at Scripture as being more literal than we ever imagined? Consider the following verses.

> *"Remember this and show yourselves men, recall to mind you transgressors, remember the former things of old, for I am God and there is no other; I am God, and there is none like me. Declaring the end from the beginning and from ancient times things that are not yet done, Saying my counsel shall stand and I will do all my pleasure."*
> *- Isaiah 46:8-10*

Obviously no true believer would have a problem taking this statement literally. God can tell us how the end will be before it happens. Simple enough! Yet, I will suggest that most believers have never considered just how literal this statement really is. What I mean by this is, because He is God, and because there is no other, and because He is the One who planted all good seed in the beginning, He alone is able to declare the end from the beginning. He knows what those seeds will produce even before they bear fruit.

If we accept this as true, and if we believe that this present generation is living in the end, then we must also accept that much of what we are currently witnessing on the world scene was *planted* in the beginning. Furthermore, the phrase "the beginning" (Heb. ראשית *reshiyt*) must be taken quite literally and should be understood to mean "Genesis."

In Hebrew the first book of the Bible is called בראשית *B'reshiyt*, which simply means "in the beginning." Because the Father declared the end from "the beginning," it seems logical to assume that, by studying the book of Genesis, we can discover what the end times should look like. Bear in mind that, as this study is conducted, we must be cognizant of the possibility that the literal text may actually be supported by what is concealed beneath the surface of the text - the seed for everything is already there. With that in mind, let us go back to the beginning - back to the book of Genesis - and see if there is anything relevant to our study that students of the Bible, both clergy and laity, may have overlooked.

THE SUBTLE SERPENT

If the parable of the wheat and tares is, as I have suggested previously, an overview of history, then it reveals not only the end but the beginning of the age. In other words, the parable reveals things that happened at about the time man was first placed in the garden (the field) to "till" or work the ground (Gen. 2:5). In the beginning we are told that man's primary purpose in the Garden was to "tend and keep it" (Gen. 2:15). The Hebrew word translated as "tend" is the same word used in Genesis 2:5 translated as "till." The word, עבד *avad*, conveys the idea of working the ground so that all the plants and herbs of the field will produce their respective fruit. In other words, man was placed there to do what was necessary for all the seed concealed beneath the surface to grow. He was aided in this endeavor by the Creator who had provided the seed, the ground and the water whereby the seed could flourish and fruit would abound.

When it comes to God's directive to "keep" the garden, a question arises - what does that mean? Most commentators suggest that it means Adam was to keep it from growing wild. That sounds logical enough but perhaps the implications do not end there. The Hebrew root word translated as "keep" is שמר *shamar*, which more literally means "to guard." If the man is actually instructed to "guard" the garden, then it must be asked - "Guard it from what - or who?"

Remember that according to the parable of the wheat and tares, the Adversary sowed his degenerate seed in God's field while "men slept" (Mt. 13:25), in other words, not at their post. Therefore, is it possible that Adam was told to guard the garden against an adversary who might want to slither in and disrupt Paradise? Is it also possible that at some point he failed to either detect or stop that intruder, consequently allowing something into the garden that God never intended to be there? Before you discount this as impossible, consider that the serpent was the most "cunning" of all the beasts of the field (Gen. 3:1).

According to Rabbinic legend, the serpent (Heb. נחש *nachash*) in its original state had the power of speech and its intellectual powers exceeded those of all other animals. Yet, it was the basest of emotions - the envy of Adam - that prompted the serpent to plot man's downfall. When did his scheme begin? More than likely, it was long before the serpent ever initiated a conversation with the man's wife. Thus, it is crucial to emphasize the serpent's cunning, his motive and his methodology if we are to more fully understand what happened. Furthermore, the details of what occurred in the beginning will better equip us to more accurately discern and interpret events in the end of days.

As far as his cunning is concerned, allow me to say that, without the guidance of the Holy Spirit, you and I would be no match for the serpent in a battle of wits. On the other hand, because of man's sin in the garden, humanity has inherited a measure of that same cunning. In other words, because of man's transgression of God's Law, the nature of mankind has in some ways come to resemble the ways of the serpent.

The Hebrew word translated as "cunning" is עָרוּם *arum*. This term is also translated as "clever, mischievous, crafty" and "subtle." Seeming simplicity is often the most dangerous weapon of cunning. The stealthy movements of a serpent are the perfect description of subtlety. In fact, עָרוּם *arum* comes from a root word (עָרַם *aram*) that means "to be (or make) bare" in the sense of being smooth and is used almost always in a derogatory sense. In other words, this Hebrew term would be similar to our idea of someone who is "slick" - slick being smooth but in an untrustworthy way. Maybe this helps explain how the serpent could have gotten past the garden's sentinel. Perhaps to Adam the serpent didn't *seem* dangerous.

Stemming from this same root word (עָרַם *aram*) is the Hebrew term translated as "naked." When Adam and Eve realized they were naked (Gen. 3:7, 10-11), the Hebrew word used is עֵירֹם *eirom*. This is why I believe man began to imitate certain attributes of the the serpent. Not only did they see they were bare in a literal sense, but as time would tell, mankind became cunning, crafty and subtle - just like the serpent.

TWO TREES, TWO SEEDS

After eating of the forbidden fruit, Adam and Eve attempted to hide from the presence of the LORD among the trees of the garden. The reason Adam gave for his stealthy movements was the fact that he was naked. You see, he was already behaving similarly to the serpent - lurking in the shadows not wanting to be detected. Notice what happens next.

> *"Then the LORD God called to Adam and said to him, 'Where are you?' So he said, 'I heard your voice in the garden, and I was afraid because I was naked; **and I hid myself.**' And He said, 'Who told you that you were naked? Have you eaten from the tree of which I commanded you that you should not eat?' "*
> *- Genesis 3:4-5*

Without a doubt God connects Adam's newly discovered nakedness with his eating of the forbidden tree. It seems that Adam had always been naked (Gen. 2:25) but had never been ashamed of it *until* he had eaten from the tree of the Knowledge of Good and Evil. Considering the lingual relationship between nakedness and subtlety as described above, is it possible that when he ate that deadly fruit, the man realized *more* than the fact that he wasn't wearing clothes? In other words, was it the act of disobedience that caused their eyes to be opened, or was there something in the fruit that caused the man and his wife to become "naked" or shall I say, "cunning"? Let us probe a bit further.

"And out of the ground the LORD God made every tree grow that is pleasant to the sight and good for food. The tree of life was also in the midst of the garden, and the tree of the knowledge of good and evil."
- *Genesis 2:9*

Some people would read this and arrive at the conclusion that God made *every* tree to grow. Certainly, we understand that God alone has the power to create, that is, to cause something to come from nothing. However, the Scripture is very specific about which trees the LORD is responsible for - *all those pleasant to the sight AND good for food*. We also know that the LORD is responsible for the Tree of Life which grew in the midst of the garden. This particular tree produced a fruit that, when eaten, enabled the man and his wife to live without fear of death (Gen. 3:22). So, what was this tree and what type of fruit did it produce?

If you will recall, I recounted in a previous chapter Judaism's belief that the Tree of Life is a representation of the Word of God. The customs associated with the reading of the Torah - the Word of God - help to underscore this association. Every Sabbath morning the Torah scroll is removed from its resting place and is paraded through the midst of the congregation. It is then opened so that the weekly *parashat* (Torah portion) can be read for all in attendance.

The parchments upon which the words are written are called the "leaves." Afterwards the *sefer torah* is lifted into the air by two spindles (also called the "branches") and turned so that all the congregants can see the words just recited. Every time I witness this custom I am reminded of what the Living Torah, the Messiah, once said: "And I, if I am lifted up from the earth, will draw all peoples to Myself" (Jn. 12:32). I am also reminded that in the New Jerusalem the Tree of Life has leaves which are for the "healing of the nations" (Rev. 22:2). In the Psalms we are told that:

*"He sent His **word** and **healed** them, and delivered them from their destruction." - Psalm 107:20*

That the Tree of Life and the Word of God are synonymous there is no doubt for it is the Word of God by which man shall truly live (Mt. 4:4). Thus, we are to understand that when the man and his wife partook of this tree, they were eating the best of foods for it gave them eternal life. Now consider what was inside that fruit - the seed. Presumably this tree grew from a seed and eventually produced fruit whose "seed was in itself." In other words, if the Tree of Life is synonymous with the Word of God, then it was the Good Seed, the Word, that produced that tree and consequently its singular fruit. So then, when Adam and Eve ate that fruit they were figuratively, if not literally, ingesting the Good Seed, the Word of God.

This now brings us to the other tree that grew in the midst of the garden, the Tree of the Knowledge of Good *and* Evil. First of all, notice that it too was growing in the midst of the garden (Gen. 3:3), perhaps in close proximity to the Tree of Life but certainly not off in some far corner. The reader should recall that the tares were sown *among* the wheat (Mt. 13:25). In fact, the tares were growing close enough to the wheat that the owner of the field did not want to uproot the tare lest the wheat be also uprooted (Mt. 13:29). Both are to grow together *until* the harvest which is the end of the age (Mt. 13:30, 40).

Now consider the fact that this tree produced fruit that, from God's point of view, was not to be considered food. He plainly told Adam not to eat the fruit because to do so meant death (Gen. 2:17). Did this warning mean that the act of obedience in and of itself would result in the punishment of death? Or could it be understood that the fruit of this particular tree actually contained something deadly? Maybe both observations are correct.

If it did contain something deadly, and I believe it did, then what was it? I suggest to you that this fruit, like that growing on the Tree of Life, contained seed, in fact, the very seed that produced the tree itself. What kind of seed was it? We know that it was a degenerate one in that it *mingled* "good" and "evil," dare I say, "truth" and "lies." This seed also resulted in death, not life, and therefore we can state with great confidence that it had to be a much different seed from the one that produced the Tree of Life.

So let us summarize what we know. The seed that grew into the Tree of the Knowledge of Good and Evil was apparently sown very close to the seed that produced the Tree of Life. This other seed eventually spawned fruit that was not good for food and, in fact, may have contained something deadly. Recall that the Bible states plainly the LORD was responsible only for trees which were pleasant to the sight and good for food. It was the woman, not God, who determined that its fruit was good for food (Gen. 3:6).

These two points alone have led me to question whether God is actually responsible for this particular tree. If He is, then I am forced to accept that God intentionally planted this tree in a very conspicuous place knowing the man would see it and be curious about its fruit. In effect, I would have to consider that God intentionally tempted him. If on the other hand He is not responsible for that tree, then who is? Recall that, according to the Messiah, the Adversary came into His field and deliberately sowed a different type of seed - his own seed - *among the wheat* knowing that this mingling of seeds would defile the entire field. Based on this point and the fact that the fruit hanging on the Tree of Knowledge was not good for food, I consider it a very real possibility, if not a probability, that the serpent sowed his own deadly seed in the garden. The end result was a tree producing fruit "whose seed is in itself."

God, knowing that a poisonous seed resided inside the fruit of this tree, warned the man not to eat it. So, He wasn't *tempting* the man after all. He was *attempting* to protect Adam and all mankind from sin and death. What made this seed so lethal? If the Good Seed, the one that produced the Tree of Life, is synonymous with the Word of God, is it then possible, if not logical, that the seed producing the Tree of Knowledge is synonymous with the serpent's word? What has his word been from the beginning? It has been a mingling of the truth with a lie - Good and Evil.

The serpent told the woman that to eat of this fruit would not result in death (Gen. 3:4) - a lie. He also told her that to eat of this fruit would open her eyes so that she could discern between good and evil (Gen. 3:5) which was true. This combination of good *and* evil has always characterized both his word and his methodology. To mingle truth with falsehood, to mix two opposing seeds results in corruption. In this way, he indeed developed his own seed - his own word. Satan is, after all, the "father" of lies (Jn. 8:44).

In short, he gave birth to and sowed the other seed.

Thus, in the beginning we see there are two opposing trees each spawned by their respective seeds. In these two trees - two seeds - we see the history of mankind, for everything recorded in the Bible and in the annals of humanity can be ultimately traced back to what happened there in the garden. In these two trees and in these two seeds, we see two opposing forces - life and death, holy and profane, blessings and curses. Everything, and I mean everything, goes back to these two seeds. In effect, every aspect of life boils down to, "Whose word are you going to receive?"

SOWN IN CORRUPTION

Do not forget that this all happened, according to the Messiah, because men were sleeping. So then, did this other tree get into the garden because the man, the one to whom the garden was entrusted, did not diligently guard against an adversary who desired to defile both the field (the world) and the crop (mankind) by sowing a different kind of seed? If so, then what Paul wrote of that first man and his failure takes on a whole new meaning.

> *"Through one man sin entered the world, and death through sin, and thus death spread to all men, because all sinned."* - Romans 5:12

If Adam had been watching instead of sleeping, maybe the serpent wouldn't have made it into the midst of the Garden with his corruptible seed. Unfortunately, he did penetrate the Garden successfully. Perhaps, the serpent used his cunning and stealth to coax the man into a slumber - and then he struck! The end result was that all mankind suffered and still suffers the consequences. Take note. If this is how it was in the beginning, then this is how it will be at the end. He is just as cunning and just as stealthy.

As to the serpent's motivation for creating all this trouble, I believe it should be obvious. His purpose has been to defile what God has purposed. We have learned that according to the Torah, God views a field or vineyard sown with two different species of seed as corrupt and defiled. Again, this seems to be the primary reason for the Adversary coming into the owner's field in Matthew 13 and so we are to understand this is why he sowed his own degenerate seed in the garden - to defile the field (the world) and the crop (mankind).

When the man and woman were eating of the Tree of Life they were, as I suggested earlier, ingesting the Good Seed, the Word, in at least a figurative way. Yet, when they took and ate of the other fruit, which contained a totally different type of seed, they ingested it also, if only in a figurative sense. That means they mingled two different species of seed and that explains how the man literally defiled himself. He had corrupted himself - body and soul - by mingling the holy with the profane. For this, and because there is nothing corrupt about God, it was necessary that God expel Adam and Eve from the Garden. Furthermore, as a result of this mingling of seed, the man's offspring were sentenced to a life *literally* seeded with corruption and subject to the curse of sin and death.

"This is the book of the genealogy of Adam. In the day that God created man, He made him in the like-

ness of God. He created them male and female, and blessed them and called them Mankind in the day they were created. And Adam lived one hundred and thirty years, and begot a son in his own likeness, after his image, and named him Seth." - Gen. 5:1-3

Most of us were raised believing that we were all made in the image and likeness of God. After all, that is what we were taught. The truth is, that is not entirely accurate. In the day that mankind was *created* it was in the image and likeness of God that He created them. But when Adam and his wife took and ate of that other seed, thus defiling themselves, something changed. Not only did he realize his nakedness; not only was he subject to death, but beginning with Seth, all of Adam's offspring were made in his image - not God's. That is to say, rather than being sons of God, mankind was from then on considered בני אדם *bnai adam* - sons of Adam. In short, corrupt and defiled.

The Scripture refers to Adam as the son of God (Lk. 3:38), but afterwards God calls men "son of man" (Heb. בן אדם *ben adam*). Examples of this are found throughout the book of Ezekiel, the prophet being referred to by God as "son of man (adam)." It is not until the second Adam, the Messiah Y'shua, that someone is again regarded as the Son of God (Mt. 16:16, Lk. 1:32). You see, we are all sons of Adam, made in his corrupted image and in his defiled likeness. We are all conceived in sin and brought forth in iniquity (Ps. 51:5). We and our forefathers have all sinned and have fallen short of the "glory of God" (Rom. 3:23). Consequently, if man and the sons of Adam are going to be reconciled to God, then it requires being "born again" - not of flesh and blood but of an undefiled and incorruptible seed (Jn. 3:3-8).

Perhaps now, you realize more acutely why the Messiah came. According to the parable of the Sower, He came looking to sow the Good Seed among good ground, that is, to those who are made of dust - sons of Adam - but who desire to be born again as sons of God. He came sowing Himself, for He is the Word and the Scriptures tell us that:

> *"As many as received Him, to them He gave the right to become children of God, to those who believe in His name, who were born, not of blood, nor of the will of the flesh, nor of the will of man, but of God.*
> *- John 1:12-13*

John and other New Testament writers further validate this concept.

> *"Behold, what manner of love the Father has bestowed on us, that we should be called children of God. . . . Beloved, now we are children of God; and it has not yet been revealed what we shall be, but we know that when He is revealed, we shall be like Him, for we shall see Him as He is." - 1 John 3:1-2*

> *"You were not redeemed with corruptible things . . . having been born again, not of corruptible seed but incorruptible through the word of God which lives and abides forever." - 1 Peter 1:18, 23*

> *"For whom He foreknew, He also predestined to be conformed to the image of His Son, that He might be the firstborn among many brethren." - Romans 8:29*

> *"...to share the likeness of His Son." - Romans 8:29*
> *[Berkeley]*

The apostle Paul makes some very interesting and relevant statements in his letter to the congregation at Corinth. Notice the terminology he uses to describe the natural body.

> "The body is **sown** in corruption, it is raised in incorruption. It is **sown** in dishonor, it is raised in glory. It is **sown** in weakness, it is raised in power. It is **sown** a natural body, it is raised a spiritual body. There is a natural body, and there is a spiritual body. And so it is written, 'The first man Adam became a living being.' The last Adam became a life-giving spirit. However, the spiritual is not first, but the natural, and afterward the spiritual. The first man was of the earth, made of dust; the second Man is the LORD from heaven. As was the man of dust, so also are those who are made of dust; and as is the heavenly Man, so also are those who are heavenly. And as **we have borne the image of the man of dust**, **we shall also bear the image of the heavenly Man**. Now this I say brethren, that flesh and blood cannot inherit the kingdom of God, nor does corruption inherit incorruption. Behold, I tell you a mystery; we shall not all sleep, but we shall all be changed - in a moment, in the twinkling of an eye, at the last trumpet. For the trumpet will sound, and the dead will be raised incorruptible, and we shall be changed. For **this corruption must put on incorruption**, and this mortal must put on immortality. So when this corruptible has put on incorruption, and this mortal has put on immortality, then shall be brought to pass the saying, that is written, 'Death is swallowed up in victory. O death, where is your sting?' " - 1 Corinthians 15:42-54

Paul's brilliant insight into Torah really shines through in these passages and he makes it crystal clear that, because of Adam, all the sons of Adam have been *sown* in corruption and are in desperate need of change. All of us, he says, have borne the image of the "man of dust" - not the image of God. Yet, because of the second Adam, the Messiah, we *can* bear His heavenly image. Furthermore, because we have been born again of the Word and by the Spirit, we also have the promise that one day this corruptible body will be transformed into the image God originally intended - His image. Thus, the transformation from sons of Adam to sons of God will be complete. The death that our father Adam introduced by mingling the two seeds will be swallowed up once and for all, for corruption has been redeemed by the second Adam, the incorruptible seed, the Word of God, Y'shua.

Perhaps, man has always been capable of good works, but no son of Adam has been able to take us back to what we were before our father ingested that poisonous fruit. No, it took the Son of God to repeal the ancient curse wrought by that God-forsaken tree. Is it mere coincidence then that the Messiah became the curse and was condemned to die upon an actual tree? (see Acts 5:30, 10:39, 13:29, Gal. 3:13, 1 Pet. 2:24) As He hung there, His blood dripped from the tree and spilled onto ground that had once been cursed because another Adam ate from a corrupt tree. His blood rolled down the tree and covered the ground - the same ground from which you and I were taken. You see, it takes the blood of the Lamb to cover that which is defiled and subject to the curse of sin and death.

Four

SLAIN FROM THE FOUNDATION

"He being dead still speaks." - Hebrews 11:4

Everything goes back to those two seeds that produced those two trees. All doctrine, all theology and all prophecy can be traced to the midst of the Garden. It is there in the very beginning that we see man already in need of a Redeemer. It is also there in the beginning that we see the serpent's scheme already at work. *Everything* can be found in the beginning because it is from the beginning that God declares the end. I dare say that more prophecy can be found in the book of Genesis than in all the prophets and the book of Revelation combined. Thus, we continue our analysis of some primary occurrences at the dawn of history to see if their lessons and their secrets have relevance for our times. So, now let us turn momentarily from the two trees and re-examine a tale of two brothers.

A TALE OF TWO BROTHERS

"Adam knew Eve his wife, and she conceived and bore Cain and said, 'I have acquired a man from the LORD.' Then she bore again, this time his brother Abel. Now, Abel was a keeper of sheep, but Cain was a tiller of the ground" - Genesis 4:1-2

Cain the farmer and Abel the shepherd were conceived in the same womb, but as we shall see, were definitely two different types of people - two different seeds if you will. This becomes obvious at the start of the narrative, albeit not in the English text. It starts becoming obvious when you understand the meaning of their Hebrew names.

Cain (Heb. קין *Kayin*) comes from a word that means "to get or acquire." His mother Eve (Heb. חוה *Chavah* - "living") *got* a man because the LORD gave her one. Later on in life, Cain attempts to *get* something by taking his brother's life. Cain is a robber - he takes illegally. He is a murderer, and he is also the firstborn; a very important factor to keep in mind.

In many commentaries, the name Abel (Heb. הבל *Havel*) is translated as "vapor" or "breath." Literally the name Abel means "nothingness" but not in the sense of having no value. Its meaning is similar to reaching into the air with your fist and closing it around nothing but air. But that "nothingness" is the very essence of life, thus, the meaning "vapor, breath." Abel, then, is a picture of something that is seemingly insignificant - nothing - but is in reality everything.

While Abel preferred the pastoral life of a shepherd, Cain was a tiller of the ground, and it was of the fruit of that ground that Cain presented to the

LORD an offering. It should be easy to imagine Cain out in the field sowing, watering, and toiling away in order to get the ground to produce sustenance for him and his family. He works hard until the seed produces the fruit. He takes a portion of his harvest and offers the fruit of his labor - his works - to the LORD.

There are many types of offerings spoken of in the Torah. These offerings were required for different purposes, and they each called for certain procedures unique to that offering. One such offering is the burnt offering, or in Hebrew the עלה *olah*. The first mention of the *olah* is in Genesis 22 where Isaac, the Promised Seed, is to be offered as a burnt offering by his father Abraham. What makes the *olah* offering so unique is that *all* of the offering is to be consumed upon the altar. Absolutely nothing was to remain untouched, that is, with the exception of the hides. The skins were not to be burned but given to the priests (Lev. 7:8).

There are several other types of offerings - the חטאה *chatah* (sin offering), the אשם *asham* (trespass offering) and שלמים *shalamim* (peace offering) just to name a few. One similarity that all the offerings mentioned here shared was that the blood of the sacrifice was spilled in lieu of the offender's blood.

One exception to these "blood offerings" was the meal offering, known in Hebrew as the מנחה *minchah*. The *minchah* is identified as an offering of gratitude consisting of the fruit of the ground - grains, flour, etc. Thus, the *minchah* is a bloodless offering. The first mention of the *minchah* is found in Genesis 4:3.

> *"And in the process of time it came to pass that Cain brought an offering (minchah) of the fruit of the ground to the LORD." - Genesis 4:3*

When Cain presented an offering of the fruit of the ground to the LORD, it was the *minchah*, a bloodless gift. Understanding that blood is such an integral part of atonement, it would be easy to see why God does not accept his insufficient gift - but the flaws of Cain's offering do not end there. This bloodless gift, the fruit of the ground, was also cursed! Why such a statement? Because the LORD told Adam:

"Cursed is the ground for your sake." Genesis 3:17

It stands to reason that if the ground was cursed because of sin, then the fruit of the ground was cursed as well. As a result, Cain brings an offering that, in and of itself, is under the curse of sin and death. His works alone cannot be accepted by a Holy God. Blood is required.

"Abel also brought of the firstborn of his flock and of their fat. And the LORD respected Abel and his offering, but He did not respect Cain and his offering. And Cain was very angry, and his countenance fell." - Genesis 4:4-5

Why did the LORD respect Abel's offering and not Cain's? When Abel offered the firstling of his flock, it is presumed that this lamb was going to be slaughtered and its carcass placed on an altar as a burnt offering - an *olah*. Based on what we have learned, it seems clear that this distinction between his and his brother's offering answers the question, not to mention that Cain's offering is cursed; Abel's is not.

While these points are all true, there is another very important detail that we need to understand, but which is not so obvious when we read the account in

English. If Abel brings a blood offering - which he does - and Cain brings a cursed and bloodless offering - the fruit of the ground, *minchah* - why does the Hebrew text say that the LORD "did not respect Cain and his *minchah*" but He did "respect Abel and his *minchah*"? In other words, though the Bible clearly identifies Abel's gift as being a lamb offered as a sacrifice (which would produce blood), God nevertheless accepts Abel's *bloodless* offering. What in the world is the text trying to say?

Notice that the text says that "Abel ALSO brought" not that, "Abel INSTEAD brought." That is a very important word in the text if we are to understand what the Scripture is hinting at. If Abel ALSO brought a lamb, it must mean that he offered something in addition to the lamb mentioned. The only other gift mentioned in the text is the *minchah* - the fruit of the ground - which, remember, is under the curse of sin and death. Yet, this is the gift that the Bible says God respected and deemed acceptable. Why?

"By faith Abel offered to God a greater sacrifice than Cain, through which he obtained witness that he was righteous, God testifying of his GIFTS; and through it he being dead still speaks" - Hebrews 11:4

While the text says that Abel offered a "greater sacrifice," the Greek word used here simply means that he offered "more," as in more than one, perhaps. The text goes on to plainly state that God testified of his "gifts" as opposed to "gift." How does the writer of Hebrews know that he presented gifts? Because as a student of the Torah, he understands the methods of study employed by his people for centuries (i.e. *peshat, remez, d'rush* and *sod - Pardes*).

Even though the text does not emphatically state that Abel brought an offering of the fruit of the ground, it seems clear that he did because why else would the Scripture say that God respected Abel's *minchah*? Yes, Abel brought the *minchah* offering, but in addition to the fruit of the ground he ALSO brought a lamb from the flock to be sacrificed. Why?

I believe it is because Abel understood that to approach God meant that one must do so humbly and with a pure heart. Abel understood that the fruit of the ground was cursed because, through his father, a curse was upon the land itself. He understood that, at best, all we have to offer in our flesh - our deeds, our works, our obedience etc. - is subject to that curse. Consequently, Abel understood that mankind was in need of a Redeemer, so not only did he bring the fruit of the earth, his works, but he also brought a lamb.

According to the author of Hebrews, he acted by faith and placed his trust in the blood of that lamb. The blood of an innocent sacrifice would cover the fruits that served as reminders of man's disobedience. By his actions, he was acknowledging that, without the shedding of blood, there is no remission for sin (Heb. 9:22). This is why he is called righteous, for at the very beginning of time, he had opened his heart to receive the only good seed which produced the fruits of righteousness. His name may mean "nothingness" but his life testifies of everything.

Perhaps this is the reason Messiah referred to him as "righteous Abel" (Mt. 23:35). The basis of his righteousness is not that he *did* good works or, shall I say, obeyed Torah, but that *it was in his heart* to do Torah the right way. Because of his faith in redemption and a redeemer, Abel knew that blood, wherein resides the life of all flesh, was required to cover that which was cursed. In short, Abel, by faith, trusted in the blood of a lamb, and as a result God respected his temporal earthly offering, the *minchah* - his works.

FATHER KNOWS BEST

Where did Abel learn of this need for redemption, considering there was no written Torah to read? I believe the Bible, in veiled fashion, points to his father Adam who learned it directly from the Heavenly Father. In order to comprehend the basis for this hypothesis, we must once again call upon the methods of study addressed earlier.

When Adam and Eve hid from the presence of the LORD, they attempted to conceal their newly discovered nakedness with fig leaves. Adam knew that their indiscretion would result in severe consequences, so he and the woman hid among the trees of the garden. Perhaps by hiding he was trying to delay the inevitable death sure to come. Had not the LORD said, "For in the day that you eat of it, you shall surely die" (Gen. 2:17)?

When God found them, He judged them for their actions. He expelled them and separated them from His Presence as a consequence, and He cursed the ground so Adam would remember on a daily basis what his disobedience had cost him. These were grave consequences that would, in 930 years, result in his physical death. Yet on that day, God did not destroy him and the woman. To the contrary, He displayed true justice - stern judgment tempered with unmerited mercy. Where is the evidence of this mercy? It is found in the promise of a Redeemer (Gen. 3:15), and epitomized in an act of benevolence when He gave them clothes to cover their nakedness.

"Also for Adam and his wife the LORD God made tunics of skin, and clothed them." - Genesis 3:21

This is incredible when you consider that their actions warranted death. True, they were expelled from the garden, and yes, they bore the consequences for their actions - the eventual death wrought by sin. Nevertheless, one cannot ignore the fact that God displayed compassion on them and "clothed them." In fact, rabbinic commentary teaches that the root word (לבש *l'vush*) of the Hebrew phrase "and clothed them" (וילבשם *vayalbishem*) is related to another phrase (לבשה *lo bushah*), which is "without shame." It seems obvious then that by clothing them the Father was displaying compassion and promising redemption in the midst of their failure.

This action not only speaks of covering the shame of sin, but it also hints to us what it cost to cover their shame. By that I mean, an animal had to die in order for there to be skins with which to clothe them. An innocent living thing gave up its life in order for them to be clothed. Recall that among the different types of offerings the Bible teaches of, the burnt offering or *olah* was the only offering where the entire carcass is consumed *with the exception of the skins* (Lev. 7:8). These skins were reserved for the priest. I should also point out that the *olah* was an offering for the atonement of sin (Lev 1:4).

It seems then that Adam, who heretofore had been given dominion over the earth and had functioned in the role of priest, by committing his act of disobedience, was disqualified from performing any priestly function. It became necessary, therefore, that God Himself step into the role of High Priest and offer a blood sacrifice for the remission of man's sin. It is conceivable that this original offering was the *olah* or burnt offering, except in this unique case, the High Priest did not keep the skins of the sacrifice but gave them to the man to cover his shame. Consequently, at the beginning of human history, the Scripture teaches us of man's inability to meet God's standards in a fallen state. He then becomes our High Priest, and only then is redemption made possible.

When Adam and Eve left the garden, they had learned several things. They knew that when God said, "Don't eat that," He meant it. They knew that disobedience resulted in breach of relationship and eventual death. They also understood that our Heavenly Father is merciful, compassionate and faithful to redeem His fallen Creation. Finally, they understood that, as a matter of protocol, sinful man cannot enter back into relationship with a Holy God without the shedding of blood.

Presumably Adam conveyed all of these truths to *both* of his sons - Abel *and* Cain. If Abel knew from his father that blood was required to cover that which is under the curse of sin and death, then Cain also knew. So, what does this say about Cain, and what does this say about Abel? Of Abel, it is a testament to the righteous seed.

THE RIGHTEOUS SEED

The writer of Hebrews says of righteous Abel, "He being dead still speaks" (Heb. 11:4), and I would add that he speaks to us in volumes. His righteousness echoes through time to teach this generation just what God regards as acceptable behavior. His example demonstrates the difference between those who act out of religious routine and those who are motivated by faith. By the way, we see that in the very beginning, faith, not law, was the basis of righteousness. Nonetheless, Abel does not disregard God's lawful standards. He obediently pursues holiness, because he pursues a Holy God.

> *"Speak to all the congregation of the children of Israel, and say to them: You shall be holy, for I the LORD your God am holy." - Leviticus 19:2*

The Hebrew word translated as "holy" is קדוש *kadosh* and comes from a root that means "to be set apart." In human terms, the concept of being holy is not intended to breed spiritual superiority, but spiritual peculiarity. To be set apart - to be holy - speaks of being different from the nations. This distinction is a hallmark of those who pursue God, because He is holy. He is set apart from the gods of the nations, therefore, his people must emulate Him, not their neighbor, not even their brother.

Holiness, according to the Holy One, is a law that discerns between the unclean and clean (Lev. 11:47). Regardless of the issue - whether it be foods, holy days or *how you sow a field* (Lev. 19:19) - holiness is the line of demarcation between what God considers acceptable and unacceptable. Unacceptable sacrifices are considered unholy.

According to the Torah, when an individual approached the LORD with a sin offering or a burnt offering and presented a disfigured animal, it was disqualified. Why? Because God is Holy! The entire book of Leviticus is inundated with the specifics of what is acceptable to God and what is not. In short, regardless of the reason, when you come to God you come His way.

Abel understood this principle and more importantly, he acknowledged God's holiness. He knew that he couldn't offer God cursed fruit alone, so motivated by faith, he brought the first fruits of his lambs, presumably to be slaughtered and offered upon an altar. The essence of his actions so long ago speaks to us today of the need for the blood of the Lamb. Abel, though dead, teaches us that our works, our good deeds, our obedience to God's laws is not enough. If we follow the Torah to the letter, if we understand all the mysteries of the Torah and yet disregard that we are in need of a Redeemer, then all we have done is to present God the fruit of our labor, subject to the curse of sin and death.

Our works, in and of themselves, are STILL subject to the curse of sin and death. Alone, our works are not and will never be enough. Blood must be shed in order to cover that which has been cursed, because without the shedding of blood there is no remission of sins (Heb. 9:22). So then, are we to ignore God's laws? In the words of Paul, "God forbid!"

Abel certainly did not ignore the need for presenting ourselves, our works and our obedience unto God. To the contrary, Abel personifies the truly righteous seed by teaching that when we acknowledge we are unable to redeem ourselves; when we consider ourselves as "nothingness"; when our faith is in the Lamb whose blood was shed for our redemption, *then*

God has respect unto our works. He accepts our acts of obedience *because* the blood of the Lamb covers the curse. This is the essence of life abundant - obedience motivated by faith in the Redeemer. This is what the Torah teaches - the Lamb slain from the foundation of the world! This is what Abel teaches us from the beginning and that is perhaps why the Lamb of God reaffirmed Abel's righteousness just days before His own death (Mt. 23:35).

Now, ladies and gentlemen - if this truth is important enough to be the hidden wisdom in the beginning, the very foundation of all that is true, then it is going to be the most important issue in the last days as well. God declares the end from the beginning. He teaches us the characteristics of the Righteous Seed in the beginning so that we can understand who the Righteous Seed are in the end. Our lesson is not complete, however. Let us now turn our attention to the other brother - the other seed - and learn what his life has to teach us.

FIVE

THE SERPENT'S SEED

"He was a murderer from the beginning." - John 8:44

If Abel's actions testify of his righteousness, then Cain's action, and to a large degree his inaction, exposes his wickedness. It should be clear by now *why* the LORD did not respect Cain's *minchah* offering - he failed to acknowledge the need for a redeemer. It seems evident that Cain was well aware that God required blood for the remission of sin, and yet he refused to act in this manner. This inaction to do what is right and acceptable is indicative of a rebel, for the Scripture teaches that:

> *"To him who knows to do good and does not do it, to him it is sin." - James 4:17*

We have no way to be certain of when and where this rebellion began to take hold in Cain's heart.

Nevertheless, it seems logical to suggest that Cain's transformation from innocent child to murderer did not happen overnight. A seed needs time to germinate and grow before blossoming into fruit, so there is no hint of trouble in the narrative until the LORD accepts Abel's offering and rejects Cain's.

> *"But He did not respect Cain and his offering. And Cain was very angry, and his countenance fell."*
> — *Genesis 4:5*

Obviously, Cain's jealousy is fueled by the fact that Abel has been blessed by God's acceptance of his "more excellent sacrifice," and according to the Hebrew wording, his jealousy boils over into a rage. It is interesting to note that the Hebrew word for "jealous (קנא *kana*) is very similar to the root word (קנה *kanah*) from which the name קין *kayin* Cain is derived. But why is he so incensed if he knows what is acceptable and what is not? Adam had certainly not taught him, the firstborn, differently from his younger brother. Even God questions his unwarranted hostility.

> *"So the Lord said to Cain, 'Why are you angry? And why has your countenance fallen? If you do well, will you not be accepted? And if you do not do well, sin lies at the door. And its desire is for you, but you should rule over it' "* — *Genesis 4:6-7*

God seems to be saying, "Cain. You have been taught righteousness, what is acceptable and what is not. Why won't you do the right thing? If you do, I will accept your offering as well! Be careful Cain. Sin is crouching at the door, waiting to pounce on you if you do not arrest the evil inclination in your heart."

There is another interesting and very reasonable interpretation of this particular passage of Scripture that comes to us from the Biblical commentator Adam Clarke (1715 - 1832). Clarke raises the possibility that the Hebrew phrase רבץ חטאת לפתח *lapetach chatat robetz* - "sin lies at the door" - should actually be rendered "a sin offering lies couched at the door." This suggestion is very credible because the term חטאת *chatat* - translated here as "sin" - is used more than one-hundred times in the Hebrew text to denote a "sin offering."

If this is the more accurate translation, the ramifications are enormous. Instead of telling Cain, "Sin is ready to pounce on you," God is telling Cain that he should not be dismayed, the sin offering is accessible; it is waiting at his door. If he would only appropriate this sacrifice, his *minchah* - his works - would be accepted. It seems that Cain's error was not in bringing the *minchah*, but in *not* taking advantage of the sin offering - the lamb ready to be slain on his behalf!

Instead, he went into the field and murdered his brother. With this barbarous act, he blatantly dismissed God's admonition and was subsequently cursed, all because he would not confess the need for a redeemer. When Cain violently rejected the blood of the Lamb, the seed of the knowledge of good and evil had borne fruit. Tares were growing among the wheat.

A MURDERER FROM THE BEGINNING

> *"Now Cain talked with Abel his brother; and it came to pass, when they were in the field, that Cain rose up against Abel his brother and killed him."*
>
> *- Genesis 4:8*

Even though the Hebrew text should be translated as, "And Cain said unto Abel his brother . . ." the Bible provides no details of the conversation. The *Syriac* text says, "Let us go to the desert." The *Latin Vulgate* records "Let us walk out." The *Septuagint* and the *Samaritan* versions say, "Let us walk out into the field." The two *Chaldee Targumim* and the *Coptic* version have similar readings. Yet, all translations record that Cain, true to his name, seeks "to get" by first plotting and then committing the world's first murder - his own brother being the victim.

Clarke observed that, "It is not merely a death ... but a violent one. It is not the death of an ordinary person, but of the most holy man then in being." As terrible as that is, tradition says that Cain was so possessed with rage that, after slaughtering Abel, he took his lifeless body, threw it on the same altar previously used by Abel and burned his body as if to say "Ok God. You want a burnt offering? Here it is!" Cain introduced murder in a most barbaric fashion. This extreme butchery is even more interesting when you consider that the Messiah, speaking of Satan, says:

"He was a murderer from the beginning." - Jn 8:44

Think about this carefully. The Messiah's statement establishes that Satan and no other is the origin of murder, yet Cain is the first murderer. Is it possible then, that Cain is merely Satan's willing operative? Permit me to suggest that it is through Adam's first-born that the Adversary successfully manifests *his* evil desires in the world and consequently provides insight into his ultimate goal, which we will discuss in greater detail shortly. We must therefore conclude that, at some point, Satan was able to influence Cain in such a way that a direct link exists between the two. That being so, we must pose the question, "How was this link established and for what purpose?" The Scripture seems to answer it this way.

> "Little children, let no one deceive you. He who practices righteousness is righteous, just as He is righteous. He who sins is of the devil, for the devil has sinned from the beginning. For this purpose the Son of God was manifested that He might destroy the works of the devil. Whoever has been born of God does not sin, for His seed remains in him; and he cannot sin because he has been born of God. In this the children of God and the children of the devil are manifest: Whoever does not practice righteousness is not of God, nor is he who does not love his brother. For this is the message that you heard from the beginning, that we should love one another, not as Cain who was of the wicked one and murdered his brother. And why did he murder him? Because his works were evil and his brother's righteous."
>
> - 1 John 3:7-12

There is a wealth of critical information contained within these passages that must be noted. First of all, John reaffirms what has already been expressed earlier. Those who have the Good Seed - the Word - within them are the children of God and exhibit this truth by producing the fruit of righteousness. Their fruit is an expression of that Good Seed and actually contains that same Good Seed, because seed produces after its own kind.

In sharp contrast are those who do not have the

Good Seed growing within them. John refers to them as "the children of the Devil," the seed of the serpent. They do not practice righteousness because they cannot - they do not have the right seed. In fact, John points out this is how we are to distinguish the children of God from the children of the devil. God's Seed is within His own and Satan's seed is within his own.

This begs the question then, "What is Satan's seed?" Considering that God's seed is His Word, is it logical to conclude that Satan's seed is his word implanted within his children who are then disseminated throughout the world? Is it not that his word *and* his children are the tares growing among the wheat? If this is so, *and this point is critical*, it means that any other "holy" book or any other writing that ignores, disputes or defies the Word of God is the word of Satan. Consequently, those who receive and embrace this degenerate seed are the Serpent's Seed.

This prompts another question. What exactly is Satan's word? Is it not a small measure of truth that is *mingled* with a lie? Consider how the serpent, the most cunning of all the beasts of the field, beguiled the woman. He took a bit of truth, mingled it with a lie and persuaded her that the intention of God's instructions was the opposite of what God had truly purposed. In other words, the reason for God's directive not to eat of the Tree of Knowledge of Good and Evil was to sustain life and to propagate the Good Seed. As long as they were eating the fruit from the Tree of Life, that Good Seed was in them. Yet, the mingling of truth and falsehood succeeded in defiling that purpose. When she ate and then persuaded her husband to eat the forbidden fruit, the result was that another seed began to germinate within them.

That seed was at odds with the Good Seed, thus defiling the man and his wife. As a consequence, God's purpose for man was compromised; two different species of seed had been willingly received and as a consequence they had to be cut off from the Tree of Life. As I noted earlier, this was and is the serpent's reason for sowing his poisonous word. This is why he sowed tares among the wheat - to corrupt and defile.

If Satan's word is his seed, then that seed is going to develop distinctly different fruit from that of the Good Seed. If the Word of God produces fruit characterized by love, mercy, faith, life, truth, etc., it will be at enmity with fruit characterized by hate, terror, intimidation, murder and lies. That fruit is produced by a different seed that originates from a source other than the God of Israel. (To him who has an ear, let him hear.) Now, this brings us back to Cain.

By what we have concluded thus far, it should be observed that John tells us much more about Cain that what meets the eye. Even though he was Abel's brother, born of the same womb, he was nevertheless of a different seed. Cain was of "the wicked one," the serpent, while righteous Abel was of God. Why? Cain's fruit proves what seed was in him, and likewise, Abel's fruit provides evidence of the seed that was in him. The fruit will reflect the seed, whether it's good or bad. Whatever the fruit is, that's what the seed is. No one has bitten into a apple and found a peach pit, for that would defy the laws of nature. In the same way, one who exhibits jealousy, hatred, falsehood and murder cannot claim to be born of God.

It must be understood that we are not speaking in terms of natural spawn. To say that Abel was born of God is simply to echo what John says of all those who are "children of God." We are made such if His seed is within us. Likewise, that Cain is of the "wicked one" is not to say that the serpent and Eve had sexual relations. To the contrary, the Scripture makes it clear that Adam had relations with his wife and she conceived and bore two sons - first Cain and then Abel. Cain was fathered by Adam, and yet in terms of his actions and whose nature he emulated, no one can deny he was born of the Adversary. At some point, Satan successfully introduced his word - the bad seed - into Cain's life, and Cain willingly received it. This would explain how Satan influenced Cain. Let us now discuss why.

METHODS BEHIND THE MADNESS

"The spirit of the wicked one in his followers impels them to afflict and destroy all those who are partakers of the Spirit of God." - Adam Clarke

In his first epistle, John informs us the reason for Abel's murder at the hand of his brother was because Cain's rebellious "works were evil and his brother's righteous." It has also been pointed out that jealousy contributed to Abel's murder. There is still another factor to consider in this tragedy. Cain killed his brother knowing that his brother had behaved righteously, and that in itself incited Cain. The favor of God upon Abel's behavior is further reason for this one born of "the wicked one" to become furious. In short, Abel's murder is the result of Cain's refusal to acknowledge what his brother testifies of; that mankind is in need of a redeemer. In effect, it is Abel's trust in the blood of a lamb that drives Cain to madness. It was this faith that attracted God's favor, and for this reason, Cain lashed out in opposition. However, it was not only Cain lashing out. By killing the righteous seed, Cain simply obliged his "father's" wishes.

By presenting the fruits of his labor AND placing faith in a future redemption, Abel posed a great threat to the designs of the enemy, and for this reason he, along with all the righteous seed to follow, was targeted for death. In essence, the first bloodshed was a religious war between two brothers, but not just any religious war. It identifies the struggle that is destined to continue until "the kingdoms of this world have become the kingdoms of our Lord and of His Messiah" (Rev. 11:15). The importance of this point should not be underestimated. God reveals the end from the beginning (Is. 46:10), and in the beginning we see the wicked seed attempting to destroy those who place faith in the blood of a lamb!

Another point to consider as we try to understand why Cain was influenced so is the fact that he was the firstborn. From a biblical perspective, the principle of the firstborn is a crucial factor in our story.

"You shall set apart to the LORD all that open the womb, that is, every firstborn that comes from an animal which you have; the males shall be the LORD's . . . All the firstborn of man among your sons you shall redeem." - Exodus 13:12-13

"The firstborn of your sons you shall give to me."
- Exodus 22:29

"All the firstborn are Mine. On the day that I struck

all the firstborn in the land of Egypt, I sanctified to Myself all the firstborn in Israel, both man and beast. They shall be Mine." - Numbers 3:13

Though revealed in the Torah centuries after Cain had ceased to exist, that the firstborn belongs to God is an eternal principle simply because God's Word is eternal. Cain, the firstborn of Adam, belonged to God, yet embraced and nurtured a different seed. It seems obvious that Satan understood the significance of the firstborn from God's point of view, and that may be one reason he wished to steal him away, as well as other notable firstborns such as Esau (but more about that later). There may be yet another layer to his plot to target Cain.

In purely human terms, Cain's motive for murder seems to stem from jealousy. Perhaps he thought that if Abel were out of the way, God would have to bless him - he would be the only seed and would be entitled to the birthright! So while they were in the field, he killed him. The problem with his plan, assuming there was a plan, was that it was impossible for God to permit Cain to be the only seed. He was of the "wicked one"; he was of another seed, a degenerate strain and, therefore, could not be the Righteous Seed - there could be no mingling. Consequently, another pure, righteous seed had to be raised up in the stead of Abel.

"And Adam knew his wife again, and she bore a son and named him Seth. 'For God has appointed another seed for me instead of Abel, whom Cain killed.' And as for Seth, to him also a son was born and he named him Enosh. Then men began to call on the name of the LORD." - Genesis 4:25-26

Notice that when the Righteous Seed reappeared, men began to call upon the name of the LORD. You see, Seth *had to be* born because there *had to be* a pure seed. Understanding the significance of this fact helps us to better understand what the Adversary truly had in mind when he decided to wage war on the Righteous Seed. As a matter of fact, understanding this will enable us to better understand human history as it relates to God's purposes and will sharpen our vision as we peer out into the future.

The Seed of the Woman

> "So the LORD God said to the serpent; 'Because you have done this, You are cursed more than all cattle, and more than every beast of the field. On your belly you shall go, and you shall eat dust all the days of your life. And I will put enmity between you and the woman, and between your seed and her Seed; He shall bruise your head, and you shall bruise His heel.' " - Genesis 3:14-15

Hopefully, everyone reading this book is familiar with this prophecy. Within it mankind finds hope for redemption through the coming Seed of the Woman as well as the promise that evil will be overcome once and for all. Furthermore, we see that God placed enmity, ("hatred, open hostility"), between the woman and the serpent and between their respective seeds. Though His heel would be bruised, Her Seed - the Messiah - is destined to crush the serpent's head, and as a logical consequence, destroy his entire *body*. That, as we know, is precisely why the Son of God came into the world - "to destroy the works of the devil" (1 Jn 3:8).

In order for this prophecy to become reality, the woman had to give birth to a Righteous Seed. Therein lies the key to understanding Satan's motive for targeting Cain, for killing Abel and why, with the death of the only good seed, it became necessary for God to raise up another good, righteous seed through Seth. Not to have done so would have conceded defeat to the serpent and doomed mankind. No, the prophecy had to be.

"The Seed of the woman is going to crush your head, and at best, you can only bruise His heel." So imagine you are the serpent, and you have just heard this statement. How would that make you feel? I would imagine, not so good. Would you just slither away and await your doom? Or would you, being the most cunning of the beasts, develop a well-thought-out strategy of your own. It would have to be a multi-faceted maneuver designed to at least confuse and frustrate God's plan. If you are crafty enough and maybe a little lucky, perhaps you could actually reverse His plan and assure your own survival. In other words, what if you were to crush the head of the woman's seed before he was able to crush your head? If you were the serpent, what would you have to lose?

Six

The Hand On The Heel

"And He said, 'Your name shall no longer be called Jacob, but Israel; for you have struggled with God and with men, and have prevailed.' " - Genesis 32:28

In Genesis 4, through Cain and Abel, we can observe the enmity between the two opposing seeds first developing. For that reason, and because it has bearing on the last days, the narrative should be closely examined. As a matter of fact, in Genesis 4:3, there is a strong inference that what transpires between Cain and Abel actually foreshadows what will happen in the end of days.

> *"And in the process of time it came to pass that Cain brought an offering of the fruit of the ground to the LORD." - Genesis 4:3*

Please recall that earlier we explained that the Hebrew text is to be understood on at least four basic levels, one of them being סוד *sod*, or "secret, hidden." It is my opinion that when reading the Hebrew text of Genesis 4:3, we can definitely see the concept of the "concealed being revealed" coming to life. What is translated as "And in the process of time it came to pass" is, in Hebrew, ויהי מקץ ימים *Va'y'hi miketz yamim*. Rendered literally this is, "And it came to pass in the *end of days*." Remember, God declares the "end from the beginning" (Is. 46:10), and here at this critical juncture in the beginning we have Hebrew text telling us something about the "end of days." Coincidence? Is it also a coincidence that the first murder was a religious war between two brothers?

Some commentators suggest that the phrase "end of days" may denote the end of the growing season, which would make sense, and would in no way detract from the notion that it also hints at what will happen in the last days. To the contrary, this interpretation would help underscore our notion, because the end of the growing season would be just before the High Holy days of *Yom Teruah* (Feast of Trumpets), *Yom Kippur* (Day of Atonement) and *Succot* (Tabernacles). Prophetically, these festivals speak of the end of age!

So, if Genesis 4 does foreshadow events yet to unfold, what should we expect? In Genesis 4, we see the serpent's offspring rising up violently to counter the righteousness of the woman's offspring. We can expect this in the end. This enmity exists between two who claim to have the same *father* - another characteristic of the end? We can also discern that, in choosing to influence the firstborn of Adam so deliberately and so diabolically, the serpent sought to have what belonged to God, and thus, established a pattern for other future events, which we will soon explain.

There is some evidence to support the notion that Cain and Abel were twins, nevertheless, Cain was the firstborn. There is also evidence to suggest that when God addressed Cain just before he murdered his brother, in addition to encouraging him to behave righteously, God was trying to allay Cain's rage.

"And unto thee shall be his desire, and thou shalt rule over him." - Genesis 4:7 (KJV)

Some commentators interpret this statement as an attempt on God's part to convince Cain that Abel was not seeking to dislodge him from his position as firstborn. To the contrary, the language should be understood to mean that Abel acknowledges Cain's role - "unto thee shall be his desire" (longing) - and that Cain's right to "rule over him" speaks concurrently of Abel's willful submission to Cain as the firstborn. Unfortunately, Cain refuses to listen and gives himself over wholeheartedly to his evil inclinations. When he does, he apparently establishes a precedent for some other notable firstborn sons.

The Bible does not tell us specifically how Cain killed his brother; it simply says that he "slew" him. The Hebrew word הרג *harag* (Gen. 4:8) hints that Cain struck him. The Greek term *esfaxen* (1 Jn. 3:12) suggests that Abel was slaughtered and then butchered similar to an animal sacrifice. While the Bible is vague, tradition suggests that when Cain smote his brother, it was with a blow to the head. After inflicting this mortal wound, Cain then proceeds to burn his brother's body on an altar. Think about this for a moment: if tradition can be trusted, it seems that Cain intentionally *crushed his brother's head.*

According to the *Jerusalem Targum* and the *Targum of Jonathan ben Uzziel*, Cain used a large stone to strike Abel in the head. The *Book of Jasher* records that Cain used a farming implement to bludgeon his brother to death. Though the weapon varies, all sources agree that the initial wound was to the head. This, I find to be extremely interesting in light of the prophecy in Genesis 3. God tells the serpent that the woman's seed is going to crush *his* head! What does the serpent do in the very next chapter? He influences the firstborn of her womb to kill her *righteous seed with a blow to the head!* Why? Because the serpent's scheme is intended to derail God's agenda by first striking a blow to the head of the one destined to destroy him. In short, from the beginning, he has been trying to reverse the decision pronounced upon him.

If this is the methodology the Adversary employed in the beginning, and we have sufficient reason to believe that the events of Genesis 4 are pre-cursors of end time events, then it stands to reason that this would be his scheme throughout history. In other words, if he seeks to crush the head of the righteous in an attempt to reverse the judgment of Genesis 3, the Scripture should verify this in some way.

THE TWO SEEDS OF ABRAHAM

> *"Now the LORD had said to Abram ... I will make you a great nation, I will bless you and make your name great." - Genesis 12:1-2*

> *"In your seed all the nations of the earth shall be blessed, because you have obeyed My voice."*
> *- Genesis 22:18*

If our theory is correct, then at the moment God blessed Abraham with the promise of seed, it must have occurred to the serpent that Abraham and his seed were going to present a problem for him. Through Abraham's seed, all the nations of the earth were to be blessed; the serpent's intent was to defile all the nations of the earth. Therefore, from his point of view, something had to be done.

After waiting ten years for a heir to be born, Sarah entreated her husband to go unto the Egyptian bondwoman, Hagar, and have children by her. According to the custom of the day, because Hagar was Sarah's servant, a child born to her would be considered a child born to Sarah. However, as we all know, things did not go as smoothly as Sarah thought they might. Hagar, being pregnant, despised her mistress and the ensuing animosity caused Hagar to flee into the wilderness. It was there in the wilderness that she was commanded to return, submit to her mistress and have the child who was to be called Ishmael.

Later, God made it clear to Abraham that, even though He would bless Ishmael and make him a great nation (Gen. 17:20), His covenant would be with his yet unborn son, Isaac. A year later, the promised son was born. When Isaac was weaned, Abraham hosted a feast in celebration. At that moment it became apparent that Ishmael harbored a great deal of animosity towards his younger brother. There was enmity between the seeds!

> "And Sarah saw the son of Hagar the Egyptian, whom she had borne to Abraham, scoffing. Therefore she said to Abraham, 'Cast out this bondwoman and her son, for the son of this bondwoman shall not be heir with my son.' "- Genesis 21:9-10

Now, I am not saying that Satan caused Abraham to go in unto Hagar, nor am I suggesting that the serpent influenced Sarah to offer Hagar unto Abraham. However, I do consider it possible that once Ishmael was born, the serpent set a plan into motion to influence this firstborn son just as he had Cain. Perhaps, Sarah's motherly intuition spared Isaac a fate similar to Abel's. Consider what the Scriptures have to say about Ishmael and his descendants.

> *"He shall be a wild man; his hand shall be against every man, and every man's hand against him. And he shall dwell in the presence of all his brethren."*
> *- Genesis 16:12*

> *"These were the names of the sons of Ishmael, by their names . . . . The firstborn of Ishmael, Nebajoth; then Kedar, Adbeel, Mibsam, Mishma, Dumah, Massa, Hadar, Tema, Jetur, Naphish, and Kedemah. These were the sons of Ishmael and these were their names, by their towns and their settlements, twelve princes according to their nations. . . . They dwelt from Havilah as far as Shur, which is east of Egypt as you go toward Assyria." - Genesis 25:13-16, 18*

According to tradition, the Egyptian bondwoman Hagar is the ancestress of all the Arab peoples and of the prophet Muhammad. That tradition is not so far fetched when you consider just where the Bible says Ishmael's descendants lived - in a land east of Egypt as you travel north toward Syria. That land would be what we now call the Arabian peninsula. It is from this peninsula that the Arab peoples hail, and where Muhammad received his revelations later recorded in the Muslim holy book, the *Qu'ran*. This will be discussed more properly in a later chapter, but for now, suffice it to say, there still exists hostility between Ishmael's seed and Isaac's seed. Let us first examine the bitterness that existed between Isaac's two sons, Esau and Jacob.

THE TWO SEEDS OF ISAAC

"Now Isaac pleaded with the LORD for his wife, because she was barren; and the LORD granted his plea, and Rebekah his wife conceived. But the children struggled together within her and she said, 'If all is well, why am I like this?' So she went to inquire of the LORD. And the LORD said to her, 'Two nations are in your womb, two peoples shall be separated from your body; one people shall be stronger than the other, and the older shall serve the younger.' So when her days were fulfilled for her to give birth, indeed there were twins in her womb. And the first came out red. He was like a hairy garment all over, so they called his name Esau. Afterward his brother came out, and his hand took hold of Esau's heel, so his name was called Jacob.... So the boys grew. And Esau was a skillful hunter, a man of the field; but Jacob was a mild man, dwelling in tents." - Genesis 25:21-27

Here we have the story of a woman who heretofore was unable to have children, but after Divine intervention, miraculously conceives. Instead of being overjoyed, she is troubled by what she discerns is going on inside of her. It bothers her so much that she decides to inquire of the LORD. The insight

He gives is startling, for He acknowledges that some-how two innocent unborn children are warring with-in the womb. The obvious question should be, "Why are they struggling?" or better yet, "What are they struggling over?" Considering what transpires later, it seems apparent that they are already fighting over who is to be firstborn. If that be the case, they are essentially fighting for the blessing and the birthright.

That God tells her there are two nations des-tined to be separated from her is interesting enough, for it suggests that these two nations are not to abide together. Yet, for the LORD to tell her that the youngest is destined to rule over the eldest confirms this in amazing fashion. Would this not breed animos-ity in an elder son living in a culture that bestows familial primacy upon the firstborn? Moreover, it could be argued that by telling her this, the LORD is effectively saying that the youngest *should* by Divine authority be the firstborn. This would help to explain why, years later, Rebekah is so adamant about helping Jacob to deceive Isaac and obtain the blessing reserved for the firstborn.

Notice something else that is rather peculiar. The oldest, Esau, is a "man of the field." His younger twin, Jacob, is a mild-mannered man who dwells in tents. In other words, Jacob was a shepherd. Does this sound remotely familiar? Does it remind you of two other brothers, one of which worked in the field while the other tended sheep? Yes, like Cain and Abel, Isaac's sons are two boys born of the same womb, yet it becomes evident that they are two separate peoples - two different seeds!

The Scripture says that as Esau was emerging from the womb Jacob followed him, and that his hand was on Esau's heel. For this reason, Jacob (Heb. Ya'akov) is understood to mean, "supplanter" or "trickster." The definition seems to be substantiated by the fact that Jacob deceived his father and "cheated" Esau out of his blessing (previously he had bargained with Esau for the birthright). He also successfully "tricked" his uncle Laban and thus solidified the traditional notion that he was indeed a "supplanter." Or was he?

It should be noted again that God is the one who acknowledged that Jacob was the one through whom the covenant would be confirmed, so is it right to say that he cheated Esau out of something that, in God's eyes, belonged to Jacob in the first place? Therefore, I wish to challenge the notion that Jacob means "supplanter" by simply looking at the Hebrew rendering of his name, יַעֲקֹב *Ya'akov*.

The Bible says that Jacob had his hand on Esau's heel. The Hebrew word for "heel" is עָקֵב *akev*. The Hebrew word for "hand" is יד *yad* and is represented by the Hebrew letter י *yod* (please notice the similarity in sound). The Scripture says that Jacob's hand (represented by the י *yod*) was on Esau's heel עָקֵב *akev*, so he was called יַעֲקֹב *Ya'akov*. In other words, the name Jacob does not mean "supplanter," but simply "hand on the heel." The logic of this is similar to the naming of Isaac or, in Hebrew יִצְחָק *Yitzhak* - which means "laughed." He was named this because Abraham and then Sarah *laughed* when they learned they were to have a son (Gen. 17:17; 18:12).

עָקֵב   יַעֲקֹב

Akev   *Ya'akov*
"heel"   "Jacob"

Now, that we have established what his name means, we must pose the obvious question of "Why was his hand on Esau's heel?" Was it an attempt to pull Esau back into the womb and "supplant" his birthright? Was Jacob playing the trickster even then? Or could it be that Jacob's hand was on his brother's heel to keep the heel from crushing his own head? If this is so, and I believe it is, then it confirms that the seed of the serpent has been forever trying to reverse the decision handed down in Genesis 3. In the person of Esau and in his descendants later, we see this open hostility towards the Righteous Seed accentuated.

> "I have loved you says the LORD. Yet you say, 'In what way have You loved us?' Was not Esau Jacob's brother? says the LORD. Yet Jacob I have loved, but Esau I have hated, and laid waste his mountains and his heritage for the jackals of the wilderness."
>
> - Malachi 1:2-3

Why did God hate Esau? We know that Esau, also known as Edom, was a profane man (Heb. 12:16); that he took a wife from among the Canaanites causing his parents grief (Gen. 26:34-35). He took yet another wife from among his uncle Ishmael's daughters (Gen. 28:8). Yet, the problem really seems to lie in the fact that Esau had no regard for anything holy, and by that I mean, if Esau had not sold the birthright and lost the blessing, then upon his father's death, he would have ascended to the position of family patriarch. In effect, he would have been acting priest for that family and, as a consequence, for all those of faith. But because he was profane, immoral, Godless, and possessing no regard for family honor or duty, this could not be. True to his nature, he sold the birthright for "one morsel of food" (Heb. 12:16), and as a consequence, the Scripture tells us that Esau's seed is to be spoiled (Jer. 49:10) and cut off forever (Ob. 1:10).

That God makes a clear distinction between these two seeds - Esau and Jacob - cannot be denied. Furthermore, it is very apparent that, even though there was a measure of reconciliation between the two brothers, it didn't take long for their respective descendants to rekindle the rivalry in deadly fashion. The hostility upon the part of Edom towards Jacob prompts the prophet Obadiah to declare that God would cut off Esau forever and primarily due to the "violence against your brother Jacob" (Ob. 1:10).

THE SERPENT'S WAR ON ISRAEL

Esau's descendants, the Edomites (also called Idumeans), lived in an area that extended along the eastern border of the Arabah valley, from the Dead Sea to Elat. Edomite history was marked by continuous hostility and warfare with Israel. At one point, however, Edom was subdued by the Hasmoneans and forced to merge with the Jews (2nd century B.C.E.). Two centuries later, the most prominent of these assimilated Idumeans - Herod the Great - ascended to power in Judea just years prior to the Messiah's birth. Is it mere coincidence that it was a descendant of Esau who, learning of the birth of Israel's King - the seed of the woman of Genesis 3 - attempted to destroy him? Also consider that this descendant of Esau ascended the throne of Judea with the backing of the Roman government. This point is extremely important to note due to the probability that this particular relationship

- Edom and Rome - may have set a precedent for other future events, i.e. the rise of the Anti-Messiah.

Through the house of Esau, it appears that the Adversary was earnestly trying to fulfill his plan to destroy the Promised Seed. He tried with Cain. He probably tried with Ishmael. He tried harder with Esau, and he certainly attempted to destroy God's Promised One at Golgotha. And while that was his ultimate goal - to destroy the Messiah - the incident surrounding Jacob's birth and the subsequent hostility between he and his brother should not be underestimated, for it demonstrates the enemy's intense hatred for God's people *ISRAEL*. It is Israel that God said, "shall be a peculiar treasure unto me *above all people . . .* a kingdom of priests" (Ex. 19:5-6). God said of Israel, "Israel is my son, *even my firstborn*" (Ex. 4:22). In other words, Israel is *marked* as God's seed born of a woman.

For that reason, Israel has been *marked* for destruction as far as the enemy is concerned. Why do you think that the nation of Israel and her descendants have always suffered at the hand of the oppressor? Put simply, the serpent wants to destroy Israel before his head is flattened, and that is why, I believe, Esau and his descendants after him sought and *are presently seeking* to destroy their brother Jacob - Israel.

I am completely convinced that the struggle which began in Rebecca's womb continues unto this very day. This conviction is based on, of course, what we read in the beginning (Gen. 25:21-34), but also upon what certain prophets have to say, and by observing what is going on in the world today, primarily in the land of Israel. Specifically, the prophets Ezekiel and Obadiah strongly suggest that the people the world refers to as the "Palestinians" are more than likely those who the Bible refers to as Idumeans or Edomites - the descendants of Esau.

It is the descendants of Esau that God says have taken the mountainous regions of Israel "to themselves as a possession . . . in order to plunder its open country" (Ez. 36:1-5). For this reason, God speaks against them and, according to Obadiah, promises to destroy them utterly because of the violence they have committed against their brother Jacob. (Oba. 1:10, 18). When you read both of these prophecies, it is obvious that they both refer to events in the last days.

Interestingly enough, the mountainous region of Israel comprises, primarily, the region referred to as the West Bank - the same region Palestinians claim for themselves as their country. It is also interesting to note that the Hebrew word in Obadiah translated as "violence" is חמס *hamas*. This, of course, is the name of the Gaza-based Palestinian terror group which carries out homicide bombings against innocent Israelis. In Arabic *hamas* means "zeal." The name of the organization *Hamas* is actually an Arabic acronym for the "Islamic Resistance Movement." Nevertheless, that Edom is finally destroyed in the end of days and for *hamas* against Israel no less is too uncanny to be a coincidence.

Think about this. Esau tried to destroy Jacob in the womb. If he had been successful, there would have been no Israel. A descendant of Esau tried to destroy the Messiah at His birth. If he had succeeded, there would have been no Seed of the Woman capable of destroying the serpent. Now at the end of days, there are a group of people who are aggressively seeking to destroy the Jewish people and lay claim to all of the land the Bible regards as Israel. More than likely, these people are descendants of Esau. Do you see a pattern? Do you see that the end is truly revealed in the beginning? Esau has always, and until destroyed, will always be trying to put his heel on Jacob's head.

ISRAEL'S HEEL ON ESAU'S HEAD

"Then Jacob was left alone; and a man wrestled with him until the breaking of day. Now when He saw that He did not prevail against him, He touched the socket of his hip and the socket of Jacob's hip was out of joint as He wrestled with him. And He said, 'Let Me go, for the day breaks.' But he said, 'I will not let You go unless You bless me!' So He said to him, 'What is your name?' He said, 'Jacob.' And He said, 'Your name shall no longer be called Jacob, but Israel; for you have struggled with God and with men, and have prevailed.'" - Genesis 32:24-28

There are a couple of items in this passage of Scripture that should be noted. First of all, this event happens just before Jacob is to encounter a brother who, at their last meeting, wanted to kill him. Therefore, it seems obvious that what happened to Jacob that night occurred in order to allay his fear of Esau. Secondly, Jacob is described as having "struggled" - and that word infers "power, perseverance" - with God, and because of that, he "shall prevail," which is to mean "overcome."

As a matter of fact, according to the *Septuagint* and the *Vulgate* this particular passage is rendered, "Because you have power with God, you shall also prevail with men." In other words, "You are to be called Israel, because no longer will your head be under the heel of your enemy, but his head shall be under your heel. As Israel you are destined to overcome your mortal enemy."

Thus, the mission of Israel is to be God's human advocacy for justice, holiness and righteousness and to persevere in the face of those who would resist God's agenda and overcome those who would destroy His Good Seed. Remember that Y'shua said the Good Seed, beside being the Word of God, is "the sons of the kingdom" which have been scattered by the Son of Man (Mt. 13:37 - 38). In short, Israel is the name given to God's family because they are His seed born of a woman.

Before moving on, there is one last observation I would like to note about this narrative. It could be argued that at the brook Jabbok, Jacob was "born again." After encountering One who is unmistakably the Word of God (he called the place *Peniel* - "I saw God face to face"), Jacob receives a new name that carries prophetic implications, and *he never walked the same way again!* So as I see it, the Scripture hints that the Good Seed - Israel - is a seed that has been reborn after an encounter with the Word of God. This encounter changes their nature and defines their purpose, thus causing them to walk distinctly different from everyone else.

It is this defining walk and God-ordained purpose that deeply troubles the serpent. It disturbed him in the beginning in the person of Abel and continues to agitate him today. For that reason, Satan still uses his agents to destroy *them* just as he used Cain to eliminate their predecessor. However, we also see that the serpent of old has never been completely successful in his scheme.

Though he persisted, he nevertheless failed to crush Jacob and his descendants, most notably, the One who was destined to destroy the works of the devil. No doubt, the enemy looked upon a beaten, bloodied Messiah hanging upon a tree and thought that success was finally in his grasp - that is, until three days later! And so, just as he failed to destroy their King, he will ultimately fail in his assault against the Good Seed called Israel. Still, he persists. He was soundly defeated two thousand years ago but he has not yet been banished to the abyss. Knowing he has but a short time, he continues in a futile attempt to vanquish the Seed of the woman.

SEVEN

ISRAEL THE GOOD SEED

"The good seed are the children of the kingdom."
- Matthew 13:38

Messiah, the Living Word, is the Good Seed and the Seed of the woman - of this there is no doubt. When He arose from the tomb, He conquered death, hell, and the grave and effectively crushed the head of the serpent. Yet, as we previously pointed out, the serpent has yet to be cast into the Lake of Fire. He continues in his attempt to destroy God's purposes in the time left to him. No longer able to afflict the King of Israel, the focus of his fury is the Good Seed - the sons of the Kingdom identified as Israel.

Israel, as we have learned, is purposed by God to "prevail" against her enemies; those used of the serpent to destroy her - Esau, Ishmael, Cain, etc. This list of antagonists would have to include the serpent himself since he is pitted in a bitter struggle with the Righteous Seed. So it must be concluded that Israel is destined to overcome the serpent. In effect, Israel is to play a role in Satan's defeat. That is not to say that anyone can add to what the Messiah has accomplished. Nevertheless, the serpent is still on the loose seeking to destroy the Good Seed.

Earlier we read the prophecy about this ancient struggle and the eventual defeat of the serpent.

"And I will put enmity between you and the woman, and between your seed and her seed; He will bruise your head and you shall bruise His heel."
- Gen. 3:15

Again, the "He" mentioned is none other than Messiah. It is He who will destroy the devil. However, there is another rendering of this particular passage that is worthy of comment. The *Hertz Edition of the Pentateuch and Haftarahs* translates this passage as:

"And I will put enmity between thee and the woman, and between thy seed and her seed; **they** *shall bruise thy head and thou shalt bruise* **their** *heel." - Gen. 3:15*

This particular translation is provocative and, perhaps to some, controversial, but it is also fascinating in light of our topic. Certain theologians might argue that Rabbi Hertz preferred this translation because he wanted to remove any hints of Messiah in this prophecy. While I am confident that Hertz never acknowledged Y'shua as being the primary focus of the prophecy, I tend to disagree with the notion that he purposely mistranslated it to hide the Messianic connotations.

The basis for my conclusion is the Hebrew text itself and what it hints at. Specifically, this centers around the word הוא *hu* translated as "He" in the NKJV or "they" as in Hertz's translation. *Hu* הוא is definitely the Hebrew word for "he," but it is also the word used to translate "it." In fact, that is how the Authorized King James Version translates הוא *hu* in Genesis 3:15. If you are approaching this prophecy from the perspective of a believer in Messiah Y'shua, you would be inclined to translate הוא *hu* as "He." If, on the other hand, you were approaching this prophecy with the understanding that Israel is the identity of the Righteous Seed - also a biblically sound conclusion - then you might see הוא *hu* as being "he" collectively or "it", or better still, "they."

As far as "his heel" or "their heel" is concerned, the Scripture does not specify. Translated literally, it says that the serpent "shall bruise a heel." It may be assumed that it is the heel of the one who crushes his head. So, depending on how הוא *hu* is translated, that word determines if it is to be "his heel" or "their heel." That being said, there exists the probability that both translations are correct. No one translation is more correct than the other, and that means this prophecy, like many others, has dual applications. The Messiah, the Head, is the Seed of the woman, and Israel, the Body, is the seed of the woman as well. That the serpent strikes at the "heel" may also hint at this second perspective. Remember, there is an association between the word "heel" עָקֵב *akev* and the name יעקב *Ya'akov* who, when "born again," was called Israel. It seems the Hebrew text hints that the heel being struck is actually Israel under the kingship of the Messiah.

Now we arrive at the point where we must ask,

"Who is Israel from a strictly Biblical perspective?"
Before I answer that, I must state that I vehemently
reject the lie of Replacement Theology. The Church
has not usurped Israel. To the contrary, what we refer
to as the Church is simply a part of Israel. Based on
passages such as Ephesians 2, Romans 11 and
Galatians 3, just to name a few, I consider myself a
proponent of Emplacement Theology - that is, non-
Jewish believers have been grafted into and have
become part of an already existing family tree called
Israel.

Furthermore, Israel's identity has *never been
limited* to flesh and blood genealogies but has always
been determined as being those who receive the Good
Seed, the Word of God, by FAITH! Having received
this seed, they walk accordingly and produce the
respective fruit "whose seed is in itself according to its
kind" (Gen. 1:12). It was Abel's *faith* that God
acknowledged and thereby hailed him as righteous.
Because of his *faith*, Abraham is deemed to be righteous with the result being that certain promises were
made to him and to his seed.

THE HEIRS OF ABRAHAM

*"Therefore know that only those who are of faith are
the sons of Abraham. And the Scripture, foreseeing
that God would justify the Gentiles by faith,
preached the gospel to Abraham beforehand saying,
'In you all the nations shall be blessed'. So then
those who are of faith are blessed with believing
Abraham. . . . Now to Abraham and his seed were
the promises made. He does not say , 'And to seeds,'
as of many, but as of one. 'And to your Seed,' who is*

Messiah! . . . For you are all sons of God through faith in Messiah Y'shua! For as many of you as were baptized into Messiah have put on Messiah. There is neither Jew nor Greek, there is neither slave nor free, there is neither male nor female: for you are all one in Messiah Y'shua. And if you are Messiah's, then you are Abraham's seed and heirs according to the promise." - Galatians 3:7-9, 16, 26-29

Paul could not have said it more clearly - it takes faith in the Word of God to produce the fruit of righteousness. Within that fruit resides the same seed waiting to impregnate the faith of someone else. Without faith, the Word of God is just words on paper. The Life it provides can be realized only when our faith is activated, and by that I mean we are prompted to obey God's Word because we believe it *is* God's Word. Paul is adamant about the fact that this type of faith has always been the determining factor in identifying those who are the "sons of Abraham." The Messiah verifies this truth in a blistering exchange with some Jews who believed, oddly enough, that He was the Messiah.

"'If you abide in My word, you are My disciples indeed. And you shall know the truth and the truth shall make you free.' They answered Him, 'We are Abraham's descendants, and have never been in bondage to anyone. How can you say, You will be made free?' Y'shua answered them . . . 'I know that you are Abraham's descendants, but you seek to kill Me, because My word has no place in you. I speak what I have seen with My Father, and you do what you have seen with your father.' They answered and

said to Him, 'Abraham is our father.' Y'shua said to them, 'If you were Abraham's children, you would do the works of Abraham. But now you seek to kill me, a man who has told you the truth which I heard from God. Abraham did not do this. You do the works of your father. . . . You are of your father the devil.' " - John 8:31-33, 37-41, 44

Thus, we see that if Paul's words are not convincing enough, the Messiah lays the issue to rest. Abraham's seed is *not limited* to flesh and blood, but more properly reckoned as those who do the works of Abraham, in other words, those who exercise their faith in the Word of God by following the example of Abraham. Being his natural seed does not guarantee that God views one as being entitled to the blessings of Abraham.

Recently, a friend and I made the observation that conservative spokesman Michael Reagan emulates the values of his father, the late President Ronald Reagan, more faithfully than does President Reagan's namesake, Ron Reagan, Jr. As a matter of fact, Ron Jr.'s politics seem to closely resemble those of his famous father's political opponents! What makes this interesting in light of the point I am trying to make is, Michael Reagan is the adopted son, and Ron Reagan is the late President's flesh and blood. Yet, who "looks" most like his father when it comes to imitating his principles and furthering his causes - the adopted son or the natural born son? This is the point that the Messiah and Paul were making.

That being said, let me assure the reader that I am in no way suggesting that ethnic Jewry is of no consequence. Nor am I inferring that the modern state of Israel is of little or no real spiritual significance. To the contrary, I believe the Jewish people at large are our brethren and the land of Israel is where God will assemble *all* of His children.

Paul tells us, the wild branch, not to boast against the other branches (Rom. 11:18-20). He also reminds us that some of the natural branches will be grafted back into the tree (Rom. 11:24), and soon after, "*all* Israel shall be saved" (Rom. 11:26). Speaking of some of the natural born sons, he also says:

> "*Concerning the Gospel they are enemies for your sake, but concerning the election they are beloved for the sake of the fathers. For the gifts and the calling of God are irrevocable.*" - Romans 11:28-29

Just because the Messiah redeemed non-Jews doesn't mean that the Jewish people at large have been cast off. Again, the Church has not replaced Israel and the Jew. To the contrary, our place is *with* Israel as part of that already existing Body. Though popular theology defines Israel as being natural born descendants of Abraham and the Church of the Messiah as being a separate entity, the Scripture disagrees. The Scripture teaches that the non-Jewish believers are to become one with natural born Israel. Paul highlighted this when he noted in Galatians that the Scripture foresaw God would justify *the Gentile nations by faith* and, in fact, revealed this beforehand to Abraham when He said:

> "*In you all the nations shall be blessed.*" - Gal. 3:8

The passage Paul refers to is in Genesis:

"I will bless those who bless you, and I will curse him who curses you; and in you all the families of the earth shall be blessed." - Genesis 12:3

Most of us are very familiar with this passage and the theology derived from it, but I ask you - exactly how does this Scripture reveal that God intended to justify the Gentiles by faith? The answer, I believe, evades us until we take a look at the Hebrew text. When we look at what Moses wrote, the answer to my question seems to center on the Hebrew phrase "shall be blessed" which in Hebrew is ונברכו *v'nivrakhu*. To truly understand the nuances of this phrase, I wish to quote a work by an esteemed fellow servant, D. Thomas Lancaster.

> *"The Artscroll Tanach Series Bereishis commentary cites an opinion regarding the words, 'And all peoples on earth will be blessed through you.' The opinion states that the verb v'nivracu, which means "will be blessed," is related to the Mishnaic Hebrew term mavrik, which means "to intermingle, to graft." This opinion is based on a grammatical anomaly in Genesis 12:3. The verb "bless" (barak) is rarely found in the form (niphal) that it appears in Genesis 12:3. The same verbal root, however, is continually found in this form in regard to "grafting" of plants. Thus, one might translate the verse as "All peoples on earth will be grafted into you."*
> *- The Mystery of the Gospel, p. 32*

This information, ladies and gentlemen, is ballistic for a couple of reasons. First of all, if this is a correct interpretation of Genesis 12:3, then Torah scholars understood *from the beginning* that Gentiles were to come to faith in God and be brought into the family tree, one that Paul describes in Romans 11 as an olive tree. Paul writes that we, the Gentiles, are a wild branch that is "grafted" into the main tree. Interestingly, the technical term used to describe the branch being grafted into the root stock is *scion* and means "heir." Please notice that the branch Paul describes as being grafted into the cultivated olive tree is also an olive branch, albeit a wild one (Rom. 11:24). Nevertheless, it is not a fig branch or a myrtle branch. It is an olive branch, which means it originated from the same species of seed as did the cultivated tree! Why is that important? Because the Torah teaches there can be no mingling of species of seed, or else the field (Lev. 19:19), the vineyard (Deut. 22:9), or in this case, the tree is defiled.

Based on this law, Rabbinic commentary argues, logically, that the taboo against mingling seeds should be extended to include the grafting of trees and plants. In other words, it is unlawful to graft a different species onto a plant or tree. That is why it is a wild olive branch that is grafted into the cultivated olive tree. This being understood, for the nations to be "grafted" into Abraham as Mr. Lancaster suggests, implies that they must be the same type of seed as Abraham. That they are of the same "seed" but are also from the nations strongly indicates that Abraham's seed is comprised of those who are of faith and not *necessarily* those of blood. This is a point Paul strives to make throughout his ministry in most, if not all, of his epistles.

In the end, there is only one tree, not two, in Romans 11. In Galatians 3 Paul notes that there is neither Jew nor Greek. In his letter to the Ephesians he writes:

> *"For He Himself is our peace, who has made both one, and has broken down the middle wall of separa-tion ... so as to create in Himself one new man from the two, thus making peace, and that He might rec-oncile them both to God in one body through the cross, thereby putting to death the enmity . . . Now therefore, you (non-Jews) are no longer strangers and foreigners, but fellow citizens with the saints and members of the household of God."*
> *- Ephesians 2:13-16, 19*

> *There is one body and one Spirit, . . . one Lord, one faith, one baptism, one God and Father of all, who is above all, and through all, and in you all."*
> *- Ephesians 4:4-6*

In short, there is only one Good Seed, identified by Paul as the Messiah and those who have trusted in Him.

> *"Now to Abraham and his seed were the promises made. He does not say , 'And to seeds,' as of many, but as of one. 'And to your Seed,' who is Messiah ... You are all one in Messiah Y'shua. And if you are Messiah's, then YOU ARE Abraham's seed and heirs according to the promise."*
> *- Galatians 3:16, 28-29*

Notice that there are not multiple seeds, but one. One reason there cannot be multiple seeds is because of the Torah's restriction against mingling seeds. Again, there is only one Good Seed. If that seed bears the covenant of Abraham and inherits the blessings bestowed upon him, then what is the identity of Abraham's seed? Isaac or Ishmael? If Isaac, then Esau or Jacob who is later "reborn" as Israel? The answer is obvious - Israel. As believers, we are the seed of Abraham, called Israel, because the Messiah, the King of Israel, is THE SEED of Abraham.

What this means, then, is there cannot be an entity called the Church with one set of rules and a specific destiny and a second entity called Israel with another set of rules and its own distinct destiny. If that were true, then there must be more than one good seed, and that is not what the Scripture teaches.

Let us take this a step further. If we are Abraham's seed because of our faith in Messiah, then because He is the Seed of the Woman, should we not also be considered the seed of the woman? The answer is "Yes," and I intend to make this truth more evident shortly. Why is it important to raise this question? Because, in the beginning, God placed enmity between the seed of the woman and the seed of the serpent.

If we are the seed of the woman, also identified as Israel, then the Adversary has marked us for destruction along with our Jewish brethren. The enemy wants to crush *all* of the righteous seed Israel! The very reason he has waged such a violent war against the nation of Israel is because he understands what its existence portends for him. That is what he has been trying to do from the very beginning, and it is what he will continue trying to do until he is cast into the abyss.

Allow me to re-emphasize that when the Messiah was crucified and then rose from the dead, He defeated the works of the devil! On the other hand, it is also clear that Satan is not in the bottomless pit. So, what conclusions should we draw from this? It suggests that Israel, the Good Seed, still has a role to play in the last days, and one that goes beyond what theologians have conceded. Frankly, Israel is destined to overcome her enemies, and chief among them is the serpent himself. Israel is going to ultimately overcome the serpent!

For his part, having done all he can to the Messiah, he has no choice but to channel his hatred toward those who pose the greatest threat to his domain of darkness. That means there is going to be a climactic struggle between these two seeds. Though the trials will be great and the suffering intense, in the end the Righteous Seed shall prevail. Y'shua said:

"And you will be hated by all men for My name's sake. But he who endures to the end shall be saved."
- Mark 13:13

"These things I have spoken to you, that in Me you may have peace. In the world you will have tribula-tion, but be of good cheer, I have overcome the world." - John 16:33

"Behold, I give you the authority to trample on ser-pents and scorpions, and over all the power of the enemy, and nothing shall by any means hurt you."
- Luke 10:19

He has overcome, therefore, we will overcome albeit in the face of unrestrained adversity. To prevail is the destiny of Israel, prescribed by God when He bestowed the name upon Jacob. In the beginning

Jacob had to put his hand on the heel that intended to crush him, but in the end, Israel's heel will be on the head of her adversary. It seems that the Messiah verified this and, in fact, granted us the authority to join with Him in stepping on the head of the serpent. When He said, "I give you the authority to trample on serpents," could it be He is referring to the prophecy of Genesis 3:15? The Greek term *pateo*, translated as "trample" means, according to *Thayer's Definitions*, "to crush with the feet." I suggest to the reader that is *exactly* what Y'shua intended to convey.

THE SUN-CLOTHED WOMAN

"Remember the former things of old, for I am God, and there is no other. I am God, and there is none like Me, declaring the end from the beginning, and from ancient times things that are not yet done."
- Isaiah 46:9-10

Up to this point, we have examined the principle of the seed. We have searched the beginning for concealed truths that they may be revealed. We have, I believe, established the identity of the Good Seed, both the Head and the Body, and the nature of the bad seed from a strictly Biblical point of view. Now, we will begin to turn our attention to what the Scripture says about the end - how the enmity between these two will play out based on all we have learned thus far from the beginning. The most appropriate place to start is in Revelation 12, for it is there that we find a woman about to give birth to her seed.

"Now a great sign appeared in heaven: a woman clothed with the sun, with the moon under her feet,

and on her head a garland of twelve stars. Then being with child, she cried out in labor and in pain to give birth. And another sign appeared in heaven: behold, a great fiery dragon having seven heads and ten horns, and seven diadems on his heads. His tail drew a third of the stars of heaven and threw them to the earth. And the dragon stood before the woman who was ready to give birth, to devour her Child **as soon as it was born***. She bore a male child who was to rule all nations with a rod of iron. And her Child was caught up to God and His throne. Then the woman fled into the wilderness, where she has a place prepared by God, that* **they** *should feed her there one thousand two hundred and sixty days. And war broke out in heaven: Michael and his angels fought with the dragon; and the dragon and his angels fought, but they did not prevail, nor was a place found for them in heaven any longer. So the great dragon was cast out,* **that serpent of old***, called the Devil and Satan, who deceives the whole world; he was cast to the earth, and his angels were cast out with him. Then I heard a loud voice saying in heaven, 'Now salvation, and strength, and the kingdom of our God, and the power of His Messiah have come, for the accuser of* **our brethren***, who accused* **them** *before our God day and night, has been cast down. And* **they overcame** *him by the blood of the Lamb and by the word of their testimony, and* **they** *did not love their lives to the death. Therefore rejoice, O heavens, and you who dwell in them! Woe to the inhabitants of the earth and the sea! For the devil has come down to you, having great wrath, because he knows that he has a short time.' Now when the dragon saw that he had been* *cast to the earth, he persecuted the woman who gave birth to the male Child. But the woman was given two wings of a great eagle, that she might fly into the wilderness to her place, where she is nourished for a time and times and half a time, from the presence of the serpent. So the serpent spewed water out of his mouth like a flood after the woman, that he might cause her to be carried away by the flood. But the earth helped the woman, and the earth opened its mouth and swallowed up the flood which the dragon had spewed out of his mouth. And the dragon was enraged with the woman, and went to make war **with the remnant of her seed**, which keep the commandments of God, and have the testimony of Y'shua the Messiah. - Revelation 12:1-17*

The miraculous appearance of this woman clothed with the sun is intended to remind us of the first woman in the beginning. Eve (Heb. חוה *Chavah*), means "life-giver," and the Scripture says of her, she is the "mother of all living" (Gen. 3:20). It was her seed that was to destroy the head of the serpent. The initial phase of this prophecy's fulfillment began when Adam "knew his wife and she conceived" (Gen. 4:1). Adam planted the seed within the woman; her egg received the seed. When these two elements joined, the result was life. The seed of the woman was the result of his seed and her egg.

The woman of Revelation 12 is obviously the greater spiritual application of what Eve represents. She is the mother of all living; her womb is impregnated by the seed of the Word that she might bring forth the fruit that expresses both the Word and Faith. This is why, in my opinion, the woman of Revelation

12 represents "faith," for without faith (or the womb), the Word of God (the seed), cannot bring forth life. Likewise, without the Word of God, faith cannot produce life.

> *"Therefore know that only those who are of faith are sons of Abraham." - Galatians 3:7*

> *"By faith Sarah herself also received strength to conceive seed, and she bore a child when she was past the age, because she judged Him faithful who had promised." - Hebrews 11:11*

> *"For as the body without the spirit is dead, so faith without works is dead also." - James 2:26*

Faith is indispensible in producing the children of faith, just as the Word - or as James alludes to it, works - must be present to produce the seed of promise. The Hebrew word for faith, אמונה *emunah*, is derived from the root אמן *aman*, or we might say, "Amen." This root means to "support, uphold, nourish" as a parent or nurse, and by extension conveys the idea of belief or trust in the one who nourishes you. Interestingly enough, the first two letters of אמן *aman* and אמונה *emunah*, "faith," form the word אם *em*, or "mother."

This mother, being ready to deliver, is in travail reminding us of what the LORD told Eve. "I will greatly multiply your sorrow ... in pain you shall bring forth children" (Gen. 3:16). Just before she delivers the child, the dragon appears and stands before her waiting for the child to come forth. He is there to kill the Seed of the woman, presumably, before the Seed of the woman can destroy him. Remember that the first of

Eve's sons was Cain, and Cain was of that wicked one. I am convinced that the serpent was there when Cain was born, just waiting for the opportunity to inject his poisonous seed into him.

The fact that Revelation 12 reveals he awaited the birth of the woman's seed suggests that this chapter is actually a behind-the-scenes overview of human history. It reveals the enmity between the woman and the serpent and their respective seeds, starting at the beginning and going through to the end. Of course, we know that Cain was not the fruition of the Seed prophecy. The Messiah is. It is He that the serpent has striven to destroy, and that is why John the Revelator sees the woman giving birth to a child who is destined to rule the nations with a rod of iron (Psa. 2:7-9).

John then tells us, in a manner of speaking, that the serpent cannot overcome the woman or the male Child. She is preserved in a place prepared of God, and He is caught up to God and to His Throne. Consequently, the serpent must channel his wrath toward a distinct group of people. These "brethren" have endured accusations raised by the serpent himself. But in the end, "they *overcame* him by the *blood* of the Lamb and by the *word* of their testimony." They are characterized as people who "keep the commandments of God, *and* have the testimony of Y'shua the Messiah." The Bible identifies them as "the remnant of her seed." The woman, impregnated by the Word, consequently gave birth to the Living Word. Therefore, when her remnant seed overcomes the giver of the counterfeit word, the Messiah promises:

> *"To him who overcomes I will give to eat from the tree of life, which is in the midst of the Paradise of God." - Revelation 2:7*

The male child, the Messiah, is the Seed of the woman who overcame the serpent and who lives forever. Likewise, Israel, who is also the seed of the woman, will be given access to the Tree of Life when they too have overcome the serpent and his seed. Again, Israel is identified as those who keep the commands - they have the Word - and who have the testimony of the Messiah, the blood of the Lamb. It is important to note that the remnant of the woman's seed do not possess only one or the other. They have both Faith and the Word. Faith coupled with Truth produces the one and only Good Seed, known as Israel, the sons of the kingdom.

Let us return to the beginning for just a moment. When Abel, the righteous seed, offered the fruit of the ground, the מנחה *minchah*, he was offering the fruit of labor, or works. I would liken this to keeping the commands of the LORD. His faith prompted him to present an additional offering - a lamb whose spilled blood "covered" those things under the curse of sin and death. Consequently, God respected his acts of obedience, his works. Because of this, the serpent wanted Abel - the Good Seed - destroyed.

That the serpent's objective has not changed in the last days is evident by the fact that he makes war with the remnant of the woman's seed, those who emulate the righteousness of Abel. Remember, the writer of Hebrews tells us that he, "being dead, still speaks" (Heb. 11:4). The remnant keep his commandments but do so knowing that alone, works will never be enough. Nevertheless, they keep the commands because they love Him more than they love their own lives. These are people who pose the greatest threat to the kingdom of darkness, to the serpent and to his seed. The remnant is Israel, the Good Seed, destined to prevail against the Adversary.

In the process, however, the Bible is clear that the struggle will not be easy for Israel. In fact, working through his own body of followers, the serpent will enjoy limited success in his war against the Righteous. So this prompts the question - "Who, at the end, is the seed of the serpent? Who will he use at the end, as he did Cain in the beginning, to wield his weapons of destruction? Who will he provoke to strike at head of the Righteous Seed?" One thing is for sure - whoever it is, they will not veil their intentions. Due to the fact that God Himself placed enmity between the two seeds, and because it is God who, from the beginning, declares the end means that whoever Satan uses will display an open hostility toward Israel - toward *all* Israel!

Eight

THE MINGLED KINGDOM

*"So God looked upon the earth, and indeed it was corrupt,
for all flesh had corrupted their way on the earth."*
                                                    - Genesis 6:12

Before proceeding to reveal what the Bible has already revealed from the beginning, I believe it is important that we, once more, pause and reflect upon what has been established. First of all, there is only one Good Seed, which is the Word of God expressed through the people of God known throughout Scripture as Israel. From a Biblical perspective, Israel is not defined exclusively in terms of flesh and blood, but more accurately in terms of faith.

Because His people carry His seed, the mingling of things holy with things profane is forbidden. Moreover, there is enmity between the Good Seed and the only other seed, the bad seed of the serpent. I believe it has been well established that, because of this enmity, the Adversary has, throughout history, used those under his influence - his seed - to lash out against the people of God. In the very beginning he used instruments like Cain and Esau, those closest to the people he sought to destroy. Later he manipulated members of different cultures and even entire nations to harass and murder God's firstborn, Israel.

It is these particular world powers that I now wish to examine. Specifically, I wish to analyze a singular event recorded in the book of Daniel that reveals the primary powers who have best served the serpent's purposes in his bid to destroy Israel. Moreover, this ancient event may actually hint at what group of people the serpent intends to employ as his primary weapon in a final assault against the Righteous Seed.

BABYLON, THE HEAD OF GOLD

"Now in the second year of Nebuchadnezzar's reign, Nebuchadnezzar had dreams; and his spirit was so troubled that his sleep left him. . . . Then the secret was revealed to Daniel in a night vision. So Daniel blessed the God of heaven. Daniel answered and said: 'Blessed be the name of God forever and ever, for wisdom and might are His. And He changes the times and the seasons; He removes kings and raises up kings; He gives wisdom to the wise and knowledge to those who have understanding, He reveals deep and secret things; He knows what is in the darkness, and light dwells with Him.'"
- Daniel 2:1, 19-22

Hopefully, the reader is familiar with this story recorded in Daniel 2, and if you are not, then you are most certainly familiar with the climax of the story as recorded in Daniel 3 - the deliverance of three Hebrew men, Shadrach, Meshach and Abednego. Yet, the most revealing aspect of the story, at least as it relates to our subject, is actually concealed within the dream that God delivered to a pagan Babylonian king. This incident is a classic example of the concept introduced earlier - a truth that has been concealed will be revealed in its time. At the precise moment He had foreordained, God revealed both the details and the meaning of the king's prophetic dream to his servant Daniel for the benefit of His people then and now. You see, this was no ordinary dream, but one whose implications reached centuries into the future, culminating in the end of days.

> *"There is a God in heaven who reveals secrets, and He has made known to King Nebuchadnezzar what will be in the latter days." - Daniel 2:28*

The essence of the dream is this: Nebuchadnezzar saw a terrifying image of a man whose body was comprised of different metals, each metal distinguishing certain regions of the body. According to Daniel's interpretation, these metals symbolically described the primary Gentile nations who would persecute and, to varying degrees, influence the welfare of the nation of Israel. Starting with Babylon, likened to a head of gold, the body is described head to foot with the corresponding metal, each metal inferior in brilliance and presumably in value to the one before. In the end, the entire image was destroyed by a stone which struck at the feet of the image. This stone, representing the Messianic kingdom, covers the entire earth. The advent of this kingdom signifies the end of the kingdoms of men.

"This image's head was of fine gold, its chest and arms of silver, its belly and thighs of bronze, its legs of iron, its feet partly of iron and partly of clay. You watched while a stone was cut out without hands, which struck the image on its feet of iron and clay, and broke them in pieces. Then the iron, the clay, the bronze, the silver, and the gold were crushed together, and became like chaff from the summer threshing floors; the wind carried them away so that no trace of them was found. And the stone that struck the image became a great mountain and filled the whole earth." - Daniel 2:32-35

Daniel informs Nebuchadnezzar that he, the King of Babylon, is represented by the head of gold (Dan. 2:38) and that all the kingdoms following him will be inferior, just as silver, brass and iron are all inferior metals when compared to gold. Most eschatologists agree that following Babylon was the Medo-Persians, the chest and arms of silver. The belly and thighs of bronze was the Grecian Empire, followed by the iron legs of Rome. All of these kingdoms, distinct though they may have been, emanated from the head of gold, the kingdom of Babylon. In other words, this image - this body, if you will - acts in accordance to what "the head" initiates. So then, let us briefly examine this King Nebuchadnezzar and his strange nocturnal image and see what revelations may be unearthed as it relates to our subject matter.

First of all, it seems obvious to me that this "body" described in Daniel 2 exists in order to harass, influence and ultimately destroy the other body - that is, the Body of Messiah, a.k.a. Israel. That the head of this body is considered to be Babylon, and more specifically, the king of Babylon, suggests to me that the anti-Messiah is associated in some way with Babylon, or at least that region of the world. The basis of this conclusion is this: if the Messiah is the person-ification of God's Word, then wouldn't the anti-Messiah be the personification of Satan's word? Likewise, just as Messiah is the "head" of His body, is it not logical to assume that the anti-Messiah is the "head" of this other body? If so, then he would exhib-it the oppressive nature of Babylon.

It was Babylon who, to a larger degree than other antagonistic powers, accomplished what the Adversary had long sought to do - to destroy the place and people that God deemed His. Babylon was the first *gentile* power to destroy Jerusalem, to raze the Temple and force all of Judah's citizens into captivity. Consider that the image Nebuchadnezzar dreamed of in Daniel 2 became a reality in the next chapter, how-ever, instead of being comprised of different metals, it was an image made entirely of pure gold (Dan 3:1).

In other words, Nebuchadnezzar had an image made of himself, commanding that all peoples, nations and languages should bow and worship the image under the threat of death (Dan. 3:6). Only a few of those who believed in the God of Israel refused. Later, we see that this same king is given the heart of a *beast for seven years* (Dan. 4:16)! Is this beginning to sound familiar? It seems obvious that the anti-Messiah, as head of this wicked body, will revive the Babylonian spirit and agenda, succeeding to a point. For the Scripture says:

> *"It was granted to him to make war with the saints and to overcome them."* - Revelation 13:7

Furthermore, if he is the head of that body, if he is the personification of Satan, and if he does invoke the spirit of Babylon, then he comes not to *pose* as Messiah, as some have suggested, but to *oppose* the Messiah, His people, His temple and His Word (Rev. 13:6). It is simply this: the anti-Messiah is THE seed of the serpent just as the Messiah is THE seed of the woman. As a consequence, there exists enmity between the two seeds and the "bodies" they control.

Another point to consider is this: recall that the Scripture teaches *one* of seven heads on the beast receives a deadly wound inflicted by a sword (Rev. 13:14). By the way, these seven heads are seven principalities that comprise the essence of the beast (*I believe that essence to be the spirit of Anti-Messiah*), yet, only *one* of them received a deadly wound. Is this possibly a reference to the wound that the Messiah inflicted upon the powers of darkness two thousand years ago? Was this "sword" the same sword that proceeds from the mouth of the King of Kings (Rev. 19:15)? Whatever the cause of the wound, it heals and "all the world wondered after the beast" (Rev. 13:3).

Now it must be asked - "Which of the seven heads received that wound?" It is obviously the principality that is superior to the others, for it is this head - this wicked spirit - that receives power and authority directly from the serpent of old, the devil (Rev. 13:2, 4), and who becomes synonymous with the anti-Messiah. It is this principality's revival that causes the stunned people of the world to exclaim:

"Who is like the beast? Who is able to make war with him?" - *Revelation 13:4*

In Daniel 2, it is clear who the superior power is - the *head* of gold identified as Babylon. Just as everything holy emanates from the Messiah, everything unholy emanates from Babylon. Her guile filters down into every kingdom and king associated with her, be it Persia, Greece or Rome, e.g. Ultimately this means that all who receive her poisonous influence will eventually stand in opposition to God, His Word and His people. Why? Because Babylon did.

Consider the woman described in Revelation 17. This woman, who is actually a harlot, rides a scarlet-colored beast, the same beast who is identified earlier in Revelation 13. Obviously, this woman wishes to ride the beast, and the beast allows her to do so, at least for a time. Of the woman Scripture says:

> *"The woman was arrayed in purple and scarlet, and adorned with gold and precious stones and pearls, having in her hand a golden cup full of abominations and the filthiness of her fornication. And on her forehead a name was written: 'MYSTERY, BABYLON THE GREAT, THE MOTHER OF HARLOTS AND OF THE ABOMINATIONS OF THE EARTH.' I saw the woman, drunk with the blood of the saints and with the blood of the martyrs of Y'shua." - Revelation 17:4-6*

Now compare the sun-clothed woman of Revelation 12 to this woman clothed in scarlet. The former is observed giving birth to the One destined to rule the nations - the Promised Seed of the Woman. The latter is a harlot, which means that she certainly does not receive the one Good Seed, but a degenerate seed. Frankly, a harlot is willing to receive *any* seed.

The fact that she rides this scarlet-colored beast suggests that she has received the other seed - the seed of the serpent.

Upon her head she wears an occultic epithet that begins with "MYSTERY." Once again, the Greek word used here is *musterion* and denotes a spiritual truth that, heretofore was hidden, but now the time has come for it to be revealed. The mystery? The mother of all debauchery, abominations, fornications, false doctrine, false religion - in short, everything the Adversary would want to unleash upon the world - is Babylon. If all filthiness were traced back to its origin you would find yourself, not in Rome, but in Babylon, and why? Because Babylon is the "head" of this other "body."

Once again, compare this woman riding the beast to some other women. Consider the woman of Genesis 3. She is the "mother of all living." It is through her and her seed that the Promised One would come. We see the fruition of this Promise come to pass through the woman in Revelation 12. The Woman who gave birth to the Promised Seed was faithful. In contrast, the woman of Revelation 17 is unfaithful. In fact, the word translated as "woman" is, in the Greek text, *gune* (pronounced *goo-nay*), and specifically means "a wife." She is not just a woman, but a wife who has received another seed.

Many scholars have suggested that this woman is the "apostate Church." I tend to agree. Specifically, the woman is described as "That great city which reigns over the kings of the earth" (Rev. 17:18), presumably meaning Papal Rome. The Papacy, supposedly, represents universal Christianity (in fact, *Catholic* means "universal"). That this woman sits upon many waters, infers that her influence is vast. To deny that the Roman Papacy has embraced Babylonian influence and incorporated it into her doctrine and dogma is to deny history. Can it be said of Papal Rome that they affirm God's Laws, God's Temple and God's People, Israel? If the answer is "No," then I would suggest that the Papacy has definitely been influenced by the doctrines of Babylon.

In short, this woman could very well be those who claim the God of Israel as their Father, who claim to be married to the Messiah, and who claim to have received His Good Seed, but who in reality have committed fornication and mingled the seeds, good and bad. Whoever she is, this one thing is obvious: according to the words of the Torah, she is defiled and corrupt. This unfaithful wife rides this blasphemous beast, suggesting that she has received its heretical seed. Because she is a harlot, by Biblical definition, Babylon is her mother, and the Serpent is her father. In the end, ten kings will strip her naked, eat her flesh and burn her with fire (Rev. 17:16). Why is it necessary that she be burnt with fire? Because the Torah dictates that:

> "The daughter of any priest, if she profane herself by playing the harlot, she profanes her father. She shall be burned with fire." - Leviticus 21:9

Vile and disgraceful though she may be, *she is not the beast*! She rides and cavorts with the beast and even partakes of the shed blood of God's people, further fueling her intoxication. Nevertheless, at the appointed time, God's judgment is poured out upon her, paving the way for the culmination of all things.

"For God has put it into their hearts to fulfill His purpose, to be of one mind, and to give their kingdom to the beast, until the words of God are fulfilled." - Revelation 17:17

Like the scarlet-clothed woman, everyone who would receive a different seed has Babylon as their mother. I believe that is one of the mysteries revealed in Revelation 17. Yet, there is another aspect of the mystery. Contrary to popular opinion, I do not believe the prophecy speaks of a "Mystery Babylon the Great," in other words, the epithet on the harlot's forehead does not portend the evolution of some abstract "Babylon" yet to be revealed. To the contrary, I believe the "Mystery" is about the authentic "Babylon the Great!" The mystery, then, would be: "How does a kingdom that has been dealt a death knell come back to life?" The answer to that mystery causes all the world to wonder!

A ROMAN REVIVAL?

There is an issue that must be addressed before we go much further, and that is, "What about Rome?" Most eschatologists have theorized that, because the legs of iron in Daniel 2 are Rome, then the iron in the feet of that image *must* mean that this last-day kingdom is a revived Roman Empire. While I certainly agree that elements of the beast's kingdom will be reminiscent of Rome, I do not agree that this kingdom will emanate from Rome. Why? Because a) Rome is not the head, Babylon is, and b) because Revelation 17 makes it clear that the nation ruling the world in John's day is *not* the nation that would rule in the end.

*"The angel said to me, 'Why did you marvel? I will tell you the mystery of the woman **and** of the beast that carries her, which has the seven heads and the ten horns. The beast that you saw was, and **is not**, and will ascend out of the bottomless pit and go to **perdition**. And those who dwell on the earth will marvel, whose names are not written in the Book of Life from the foundation of the world, when they see the beast that was, and **is not**, and yet it is. Here is the mind which has wisdom; the seven heads are seven mountains upon which the woman sits. There are **also** seven kings. Five have fallen, one is, and the other has not yet come. And when he comes, he must continue a short time. The beast that was, and is **not**, is himself **also** the eighth, and is **of the seven**, and is going to **perdition**."*

- Revelation 17:7-11

First of all, I would like the reader to notice that the angel mentions two mysteries. One is about the woman, and the other is about the beast she rides. He clearly states that the beast "was" (used to be) but is not present in John 's day. If the beast was not present in John's day, then how is the beast a personification of Rome? The angel also says this beast that had been, but was not in existence during John's day would ascend out of the abyss and go to "perdition." The Greek word translated as "perdition" is *apoleian*. This word shares the same root word with the title given the king of the abyss, Apollyon (*Apolluon*).

"And they had as king over them the angel of the bottomless pit, whose name in Hebrew is Abaddon, but in Greek he has the name Apollyon." - Rev. 9:11

Notice that the Hebrew equivalent of *Apollyon* is *Abaddon*, which is derived from the root אבד *avad*. It means, "to destroy, to be lost," thus he is known as destroyer. It should also be pointed out that Nebuchadnezzar is considered to be the "destroyer" spoken of by the prophet Jeremiah (Jer. 4:7). That the destroyer *Abaddon* is released from the abyss is interesting, as well. Notice that just a few verses later, four other angels are released from the great river Euphrates (Rev. 9:14). Just north of the Persian Gulf, the Euphrates and the Tigris Rivers come together and form the border of present-day Iraq and Iran. On modern maps, the confluence of these ancient waterways is called *Shatt al Arab*. At the mouth of this estuary there exists an island called *Abadan*. Coincidence? While we are considering that *coincidence*, should we make anything of the coincidence that this king is released from the abyss in Revelation *9 - 11*?

The angel reiterates that the beast John witnesses is not presently empowered (from John's perspective), and yet is. Later John will note in his first epistle that the spirit of anti-Messiah is already at work in the world - "even now there are many anti-messiahs" - which, as John points out, is a clear indication that *the* anti-Messiah shall come (1 John 2:18).

What the angel then reveals to John is, in my opinion, the source of much confusion about the nature of the beast and his last day kingdom. It is revealed that the seven heads of the beast are "seven mountains on which the woman sits" (Rev. 17:9). This, coupled with the passage that identifies the woman as the city reigning "over the kings of the earth" (Rev. 17:18), seems to make the case for the anti-Messiah hailing from Rome. The problem with this conclusion is, as I see it, the woman is that city, the beast is not. Furthermore, if we continue to read we see that the seven heads are ALSO seven principalities, five of which have fallen. Most scholars agree that those five fallen principalities are:

* Egypt
* Assyria
* Babylon
* Medo-Persia
* Greece

All of the kingdoms listed at one time played a significant role in Israel's destiny, and apparently, each of them was controlled by their respective princes (see Dan. 10:20). The angel further discloses that the sixth of these seven principalities was in power during John's day. That sixth king is Rome. The seventh is unknown, but when he is empowered, it will be for a brief period of time. He will in turn be followed by an eighth kingdom whose prince is one of the seven - not seventh - principalities. In other words, this very last kingdom - the kingdom of the anti-Messiah - is going to be controlled by either the prince of Egypt, Assyria, Babylon, Persia, Greece, Rome or the seventh unknown king. Which one?

The angel says that, "the beast that was, and is not, is himself also the eighth" (Rev. 17:11). In other words, this last king was not empowered during John's day - that disqualifies Rome. That he "is not" means he must come from the five kings who have fallen. Furthermore, this last king is the epitome of the beast, and the source of its blasphemous nature. He is the "head" of the heads, if you will.

Now consider that Revelation 18 is basically dedicated to the destruction of one particular region - Babylon. Consider also that the name written on the forehead of the harlot says, "Babylon the Great," not "Rome the Great." If the Bible suggests anything specific about Rome, it seems to be revealed through the woman riding the beast who is, remember, burned with fire by the ten kings. Historically, Rome disseminated idolatry and false religion throughout the world in unprecedented fashion. That influence is undeniably with us today, however, the idolatry and false doctrine that Rome propagated was hatched in Babylon. Rome may, or perhaps will, play a significant role in the end, but Rome is not the "head" that has been revived - it is Babylon!

Rome, or shall I say the West, may in fact sanction and, perhaps, empower the one who will be the oppressor of Israel in the last days, just as Rome was the one who allowed Esau's descendant, Herod, to rule at the time of the Messiah's first coming. It would be, at least in my opinion, logical if once again Rome in the guise of the Catholic church or Western powers were to empower Esau's descendants to be in position to place their heel on Israel's head at the very end.

A Mingled World

I have spent a lot of time expounding upon the head of the image in Daniel 2, but now we must shift our focus to another part of this body, the feet. This is necessary because the prophecy in Daniel 2 makes it clear that the kingdom depicted as the feet is the last day kingdom. So, if the feet and toes are the last day kingdom, why devote so much attention to the head?

Like the chest and arms, the belly and thighs, and yes, the legs, the feet get their orders from the head. Nevertheless, this is the kingdom that will be empowered during the last days, just before the Messiah returns to establish His everlasting Kingdom.

*"You watched while a stone was cut out without hands, which struck the image **on its feet** of iron and clay, and broke them in pieces." - Daniel 2:34*

These two feet collectively have ten toes, corresponding to the ten horns/ten kings on the beast that John saw (Rev. 13:1; 17:12). In fact, Daniel also identifies these ten toes as ten kings in Daniel 2:44. The point is, the feet and ten toes represents the kingdom of the anti-Messiah. Why the feet? Could it be because the feet contain the heel, and the heel is used to crush the head of one's adversary? In this case, the kingdom of the beast intends to crush the head of the righteous ones. While you are thinking about this point, consider this. This last day kingdom of the beast is a *mixed* or *mingled* kingdom.

*"Whereas you saw the feet and toes, partly of potter's clay and partly of iron, the kingdom shall be divided; yet the strength of the iron shall be in it, just as you saw the iron **mixed** with ceramic clay. And as the toes of the feet were partly of iron and partly of clay, so the kingdom shall be partly strong and partly fragile. As you saw iron **mixed** with ceramic clay, they will **mingle** with the seed of men; but they will not adhere to one another, just as iron does not **mix** with clay. And in the days of these kings, the God of heaven will set up a kingdom which shall never be destroyed; and the kingdom*

145

shall not be left to other people; it shall break in pieces and consume all these kingdoms and it shall stand forever." - Daniel 2:41-44

Here is what Daniel discloses about the last-day kingdom of the beast. The prophet describes it as one containing all the ferocity and strength of the preceding kingdom - Rome - and yet, there exists an inherent weakness within this realm, likened to potter's clay. Four times during this discourse, Daniel emphasizes the mingled state of this kingdom and each time he defines that as being the source of its weakness. Now considering what we have learned thus far, this is an interesting characteristic, and one that is unique to this final kingdom of man.

This mingled kingdom evidently contains all the elements of Rome, Grecia, Persia, Egypt, Assyria and, yes, Babylon - particularly Babylon. It is also a kingdom that epitomizes who and what the beast is. Put simply, the beast is characterized by the serpent's goals and methods. His goal is to undermine and defile God's purposes by destroying the Righteous Seed. His methods have always included mingling lies with the truth - sowing tares among the wheat. I find it fascinating that Daniel specifically says this kingdom will *"mingle with the seed of men"* (Dan. 2:43).

According to the *Jamieson, Fausset and Brown Commentary*, the mingling with the seed of men seems to allude to Genesis 6:2 and the days of Noah just before the Deluge. Considering that the Messiah likens the days of His Coming to that of the days of Noah (Mt. 24:37), perhaps it behooves us to take another look at the beginning and examine, yet again, the mingling aspect of Satan's plan.

IN THE DAYS OF NOAH

> *"Now it came to pass, when men began to multiply on the face of the earth, and daughters were born to them, that the sons of God saw the daughters of men, that they were beautiful; and they took wives for themselves of all whom they chose. . . . There were giants on the earth in those days, and **also afterward**, when the sons of God came in to the daughters of men and they bore children to them. Those were the mighty men who were of old, men of renown. Then the LORD saw that the wickedness of man was great in the earth, and that every intent of the thoughts of his heart was only evil continually. And the LORD was sorry that He had made man on the earth, and He was grieved in His heart. So the LORD said, 'I will destroy man whom I have created from the face of the earth, both man and beast . . . for I am sorry that I have made them.' "*
>
> *- Genesis 6:1-2, 4-7*

A great deal has been written about these particular passages and what it means exactly. Who are these "sons of God"? What *really* happened here? Without getting too detailed, I find it necessary to tackle this particular issue because it figures prominently in the basis for our book, and it hints at what the end times will look like. There are basically three views of who and what the "sons of God" and the "daughters of men" are:

SONS OF GOD	DAUGHTERS OF MEN
1) Sons of Princes	People of lower orders
2) Angels	Mankind, generally
3) The seed of Seth	The seed of Cain

The first view is, in my opinion, easily dismissed and for this reason: the Hebrew phrase *b'nai haElohim* signifies these men are considered sons of THE God, not god. The second, and perhaps most popular view, is that these sons of God are fallen angels who procreated with any human female that struck their fancy. Their monstrous offspring are the giants mentioned, these "men of renown." The problem with this view in my estimation is that, first of all, the Bible plainly says that giants were present before and after this alleged extra-terrestrial love affair began.

> There were giants on the earth in those days, and **also afterward**, when the sons of God came in to the daughters of men and they bore children to them." - Genesis 6:4

My point is, if giants (Heb. הנפלים *ha'nephilim*) are introduced into the world as the result of angels and human beings having intercourse, how do we account for the giants who were present before this happened? Furthermore, how do we explain the antediluvian giants dwelling in Canaan when Israel was coming into the land (Num. 13:33)? What about Goliath of Gath (1 Sam. 17:4)? One of the reasons that many consider the giants to be the offspring of fallen angels is the use of the phrase הנפלים *ha'nephilim*. The root of this word is נפל *naphal* and means "to fall," thus the idea that they are "fallen ones." The problem with this conclusion, at least in my opinion, is that the giants are "the fallen ones," not the "sons of God."

While you ponder these points, consider that the Messiah Himself distinctly stated that angels cannot marry (Mt. 22:30, Lk. 20:34), and these "sons of

God" most definitely took wives for themselves of these "daughters of men" (Gen. 6:2).

I am not suggesting that these *nephilim* were not opposing the people of God. I am, however, challenging the idea that they were the offspring of angels and humans, and I am challenging the theory that giants are the emphasis of Genesis 6:4. So, assuming they are not angels and they are not merely the sons of princes, who are they? To answer that, we must go back just a bit further into the Biblical record.

"And Adam knew his wife again, and she bore a son and named him Seth, 'For God appointed another seed for me instead of Abel, whom Cain killed.' And as for Seth, to him also a son was born; and he named him Enosh. Then men began to call on the name of the LORD." - Genesis 4:25-26

"Then men began to call on the name of the LORD." What does this mean exactly? Technically, it could be perceived as saying two different and totally opposite things. Yet in the end, the result is the same, and that is this. About the time Enosh was born, mankind formally divided into two camps - those who would abide in the presence of God and those who fled to a distance from Him. In other words, the righteous seed of the woman was separated from the seed of the serpent.

A marginal reading of "Then men began to call upon the name of the LORD" could be, "Then began men to call themselves by the name of the LORD," signifying that the true followers of God began to distinguish themselves from others. Perhaps this is a correct interpretation, however, the Hebrew word that is translated as "began" - הוחל *huchal* - suggests some-thing significantly different. The root of this word is חלל *chalal* and actually means, "profane, defile, pollute, make common or desecrate." Consequently, many commentators, particularly Jewish commentators, consider this passage to mark the beginning of idola-try. Maimonides in his *Treatise on Idolatry* says:

> "In the days of Enosh the sons of Adam erred with great error and the counsel of the wise men of that age became brutish. . . . And in the process of time there stood up false prophets among the sons of Adam, which said that God had commanded and said unto them, 'Worship such a star, or all the stars and do sacrifice unto them. . . . And the false prophet showed them the image which he had feigned out of his own heart, and said it was the image of such a star which was made known unto him by prophecy. And they began after this manner to make images in temples, and under trees, and on tops of mountains and hills and assembled together and worshiped them, etc. . . . So in the process of time, the glorious and fearful name (of God) was forgotten out of the mouth of all living . . . save a few persons in the world, as Enoch, Methuselah, Noah, Shem and Eber."

The *Targum of Onkelos* records:

> "Then in his (Enosh) days the children of men ceased from praying in the name of the LORD."

Speaking of the days of Enosh, the *Targum of Jonathan* says:

> "This was the age, in the days of which they began

to err, and they made themselves idols, and sur-
named their idols by the name of the Word of the
LORD"

So, in the days of Enosh, men began to profane
the name of the LORD, and as a result, those who
upheld the Name were forced to separate themselves
from the idolaters. According to many scholars, this
remnant of true worshippers were the progenitors of
the "sons of God" mentioned in Genesis 6. This strain
of righteous seed were of the pure line of Seth who
was, remember, appointed as Righteous Seed in the
stead of Abel. Tragically, in the days before the Flood,
even those of pure Sethite lineage began to mingle
with "the daughters of men" and were taking wives of
"all whom they chose."

The phrase "of all whom they chose" suggests
they did not use discretion when choosing a wife, but
obviously chose wives from those of a lower order.
That they were of a lower order is not defined by the
color of their skin or their cultural origin, because holy
and profane has never been determined by flesh and
blood. To the contrary, Seth's line was considered pure
only by the fact that they upheld the name of the
LORD and had not mingled the Good Seed with a
degenerate seed. In other words, it is and always has
been a spiritual issue. To be of a "lower order" is
understood to mean that these "daughters of men"
were from among those who profaned the name of the
LORD.

Many of those Bible commentators who believe
that the "sons of God" were from the line of Seth also
believe that the "daughters of men" were actually
descendants of Cain who, you will recall, was of the

"wicked one" (1 Jn. 3:12). In the very beginning, his heretical clan constituted the "seed of the serpent."

Bible commentator Franz Delitzsch (1813-1890) wrote, "It cannot be denied that the connection of Genesis 6:1-8 with Genesis 4 necessitates the assumption, that such intermarriages (of the Sethite and Cainite families) did take place about the time of the flood; and the prohibition of mixed marriages under the law also favors the same idea."

Dr. John Gill (1690-1771) observed that, according to Arab tradition, immediately after the death of Adam, Seth's family separated themselves from the family of Cain and dwelt upon Mt. Hermon, supposedly the burial site of Adam. The Cainites resided in the valley beneath where, according to the tradition, Abel was killed by his brother. After some time had elapsed, the sons of Seth ventured into the valley and found the women of Cain's lineage to be of exceptional beauty, and they began to intermarry.

One last source I wish to cite on this subject is the *Book of Jasher*. Although I do not consider it to be the definitive "last word" on any subject, I do find what it has to say about this particular topic very interesting and so I include it here.

> "And all the sons of men departed from the ways of the LORD in those days as they multiplied upon the face of the earth with sons and daughters, and they taught one another their evil practices and they continued sinning against the LORD. And every man made unto himself a god, and they robbed and plundered every man his neighbor as well as his relative, and they corrupted the earth, and the earth was filled with violence. And their judges and rulers

went to the daughters of men and took their wives by force from their husbands according to their choice, and the sons of men in those days took from the cattle of the earth, the beasts of the field and the fowls of the air, and taught the **mixture** *of animals of* **one species with the other**, *in order therewith to provoke the LORD; and God saw the whole earth and it was corrupt, for all flesh had corrupted its way upon earth, all men and all animals."*

- Jasher 4:16-19

For obvious reasons, I find this quotation extremely interesting. It is obvious by *all* accounts that the emphasis in the opening verses of Genesis 6 is upon the mixture of Holy and profane - Good and Evil - and not necessarily upon the giants. Whoever the sons of God were, the result of their taking wives from the daughters of men was disastrous. Why? There is enmity between the two seeds.

When Israel was preparing to go into the land of Canaan, God warned His people not to take husbands or wives from among the pagans.

"Nor shall you make marriages with them. You shall not give your daughter to their son, nor take their daughter for your son. For they will turn your sons away from following Me, to serve other gods; so the anger of the LORD will be aroused against you and destroy you suddenly." - Deuteronomy 7:3-4

The reason Israel was not to mix with other peoples was not because of race or culture, but to prevent Israel from becoming like the nations, and thus profaning the name of the LORD God. Consider what happened to Solomon because of all the strange wives he took into his home (1 Kings 11:1-4). His actions led to the dissolution of the united kingdom of Israel, the destruction of Jerusalem, and ultimately to the captivity of the Jews under the cruel tyranny of Nebuchadnezzar. This is a major issue when Israel returns to the land from Babylon (Ezra 9:1-2) and Paul makes it a New Covenant issue as well when he says, "Do not be unequally yoked" (2 Co. 6:14).

God knew then, and He knows now, that when His people are joined to those of another seed, these two cannot co-exist in mutual harmony. One of the two, either the wheat or the tare must prevail. He knows this, because He is the One who placed the enmity between them! When those who were of the Good Seed mingled with idolaters in Genesis 6, the consequence was the depraved condition of mankind that soon followed. Notice also, that the effects of these unions were not limited to mankind, but extended to include the earth itself.

*"The earth **also** was corrupt before God, and the earth was filled with violence. So God looked upon the earth, and indeed it was corrupt; for all flesh had corrupted their way on the earth." - Genesis 6:11-12*

How is it that the earth was ALSO corrupted? Because, as we have learned, the Torah stipulates that when two different seeds have been mingled together, the vineyard or the field, or in this case the world, is *also* defiled (Deut. 22:9). Earlier in the book I mentioned that, according to rabbinical literature, tares or *zunim* - the degenerate wheat - originated during the time before the flood. The reason for this belief was because, "the earth also was corrupt before God."

"Even the earth debauched itself; wheat was sown and it produced zunim, for the zunim we find now came from the age of the Flood." - Gen. Rabbah 28:8

So the earth and everything in it was defiled. That is exactly what the enemy had intended. He wanted the world and all its inhabitants destroyed. Why? Because that would undermine God's Plan and God's Word. It almost worked, except that:

"Noah found grace in the eyes of the LORD. . . . Noah was a just man, perfect in his generations."
- Genesis 6:8-9

To say that Noah was "perfect" is not to say that he was without failure. To the contrary, he is the first man on record to pass out cold from drunkenness. The word rendered as "perfect" is the Hebrew term תמים *tammim*. It means that he was found to be "undefiled" in the same way that certain animals presented unto God for a sacrifice were deemed "acceptable" - *tammim*. In other words, Noah and presumably his sons had not defiled themselves by taking wives "of all whom they chose." True to their Godly heritage as sons of Adam and of Seth, they had refused to mingle the Good Seed with pagans and idolaters. In fact, Noah was a "just" or "righteous man" (Heb. צדיק *tzadik*) and preached that same righteousness in the years before the Flood (2 Pet. 2:5).

Just as important as establishing the standard of purity among his peers, Noah's righteousness and moral character is testament to the significance placed upon those who carry the Good Seed to remain pure and detached from the profane. Imagine what would have happened had Noah and his family followed in the ways of the "sons of God." There would have been no undefiled seed of the woman, and the promise of that seed and the serpent's destruction would have come to naught. So when the Messiah likens the days of His Coming to the days of the Noah, is He hinting at more than what has heretofore been suggested by eschatologists? Is He alluding to the fact that, just as there was a remnant of the Righteous Seed before the Deluge, there must and will be a remnant of that Good Seed that endures the time of great testing? According to the Messiah it will be a time:

> ". . . such as has not been since the beginning of the world until this time, no, nor ever shall be. And unless those days were shortened, no flesh would be saved; but for the elect's sake those days will be shortened." - Matthew 24:21

If my research is thorough and my conclusions are correct, then idolatry, profanity and the like began to appear in earnest during the days of Enosh. The ensuing wickedness devolved to such a state that God regretted creating man and made plans to destroy the earth and everything in it. In a manner of speaking, God determined to flood His field. He flooded it in order to rid it of the trash and undesirable growth. The flood destroyed everything, that is, with the exception of a handful of good seed - Noah and his family.

When the flood waters had abated from the field, He took the remnant of Good Seed, sowed it into the field and said, "Be fruitful and multiply; bring forth abundantly in the earth and multiply in it" (Gen.

9:7). In other words, He instructed the remnant of Good Seed to multiply so that the field would be full of Good Seed, just as He had instructed the first man. Unfortunately, it didn't take long for the other seed to sprout up again. In fact, we see it maturing in Genesis 11 with the introduction of the rebel king Nimrod and his defiant kingdom in the land of Shinar also called Babel, later Babylon (Gen. 10:9-10, 11:9).

The reason this wicked seed eventually re-emerged is because this is the way it works in the physical world. If I have a field and decide to flood it, everything on the surface will be destroyed. However, if there is still seed in the ground, when the conditions are favorable, that seed will eventually germinate and work its way to the surface. In the case of the Flood, all the corrupt fruit was destroyed but apparently the seed was not. The corrupt seed found its way to the surface and emerged in the region we now call Babylon. You see, the only sure way to rid a field of undesirable growth is to burn the field.

> *"By the word of God the heavens were of old, and the earth standing out of water and in the water, by which the world that then existed perished, being flooded with water. But the heavens and the earth which are now preserved by the same word, are reserved for fire until the day of judgment and perdition of ungodly men." - 2 Peter 3:5-7*

Recall that when Y'shua interpreted the parable of the wheat and tares, He stated that "all things that offend *and* those who practice lawlessness" will be removed and burned with fire. In my opinion He is saying that, not only will the wicked fruit (sons of the wicked one) be destroyed, but also the very seed (and tree) that spawned them. John the Baptist taught that at the coming of the Messiah:

> *"Every tree which does not bear good fruit is cut down and thrown into the fire." - Matthew 3:10*

In the end, only one word - Torah - will go forth from Zion. In the end, there will exist only one tree - the Tree of Life - in the midst of the New Jerusalem (Rev. 22:1) and of that city John says:

> *"There shall by no means enter it anything that defiles, or causes abomination **or a lie**, but only those who are written in the Lamb's Book of Life."*
> *- Revelation 21:27*

Unfortunately, that day is not yet here. Presently, we are living in days the Messiah likens to the days of Noah when men were "eating and drinking, marrying and giving in marriage, until the day that Noah entered the ark" (Mt. 24:38). According to the words of Y'shua, and according to what the prophets reveal, the immediate future will resemble those ancient days, but apparently worse than what Noah witnessed. It will be a world where men and women will profane the name of the LORD in unprecedented fashion. They will defy His Word as never before, *eating* poisonous seed, *drinking* abominations, yoking (*marrying*) themselves with defilement and, unfortunately, the "sons of God" will defile themselves by mingling with the profane ones.

It will be a time, as in the days before the Flood, when the earth itself will be corrupt and all because of mingled seed. Of the woman who rode the beast in Revelation 17, the Scripture said she committed fornication with the kings of the earth. In other words, this woman, presumably someone's wife, received seed from men other than her husband. She who should have received only one seed carried mingled seed. As we have learned, this results in corruption of both fruit (man) and field (earth). Thus, the Bible says:

> *"For true and righteous are His judgments, because He has judged the great harlot who* **corrupted the earth** *with her fornication." - Revelation 19:2*

All of this corruption will set the stage for the ascent of the beast who goes to perdition. He will establish a kingdom that Daniel described as partly strong and partly weak. It is a kingdom that will strive to isolate and then destroy God's people. At the same time, this despotism will seek to "mingle with the seed of men." The word that is translated as "men" in Daniel 2:43 is אנשא *anasha* and is the Aramaic equivalent of *Enosh* אנוש, Seth's son (Gen. 4:26). Thus Daniel links the feet of Nebuchadnezzar's image, the iron mingled with clay, to the spiritual climate that existed just before the Flood and the demise of the pre-diluvian world. This textual affiliation strongly suggests that this final kingdom of man will be more than tyrannical, more than violent, and more than blasphemous. The nature of this kingdom will actually be what is *needed* to trigger the end of this age and initiate the advent of the Messianic era!

It is important to once again emphasize Babylon's role in this entire scenario, because not only does Babylon define the nature of the anti-Messiah and his dominion, it also alludes to the region where these things will begin to develop. We may not be able to discern just *how* Babylon will rise again or exactly *when*, but make no mistake about it, Babylon will be a crucial factor in these last days. This particular fact hints at the probability that due to global circumstances, the Middle-East region, in conjunction with *its people and their behavior*, must soon reveal what has been concealed, yet is established in the Sacred Text. Maybe the revelations have already begun.

Daniel leaves us with one other critical clue as to the possible identity and nature of this final kingdom. We know it is a *mingled* kingdom having the strength of iron *mixed* with potter's clay. Still, the original text seems to hint at something more incredible. The word that is translated as "mingled" or "mixed" is מערב *m'arav*. It stems from the root word ערב *arav* or as we would say in English - "*Arab*." Maybe God truly does reveal the end from the beginning!

Nine

THE MARK OF CAIN

"Then Cain went out from the presence of the LORD and dwelt in the land of Nod on the east of Eden."
- Genesis 4:16

Now, dear reader, we have arrived at the pinnacle of our journey. All the lengthy explanations, all the Hebrew word studies and all of the reiterations of concepts have been intended to bring us to this one climactic point. Where and to whom does our analysis of the beginning and the evidence it divulged point us? Based on what we have learned, can we, with a reasonable degree of certainty, determine the identity of the serpent's seed in the end?

It should be noted that anyone who does not have the Good Seed in them, regardless of their race, cultural background or religious affiliation, could be identified as the seed of the serpent. Y'shua told a group of Jews that they qualified as being such.

"I know that you are Abraham's descendants, but

you seek to kill me, because My word has no place in you. . . . You are of your father the devil, and the desires of your father you want to do. He was a murderer from the beginning, and does not stand in the truth, because there is no truth in him. When he speaks a lie, he speaks from his own resources, for he is a liar and the father of it." - John 8:37,44

It seems pretty obvious that anyone who follows in the path of the devil is, from a strictly Biblical point of view, a child of the devil, the serpent's seed. Even some "christians" would be considered as such. Still, the Adversary has always managed to find a particular person or a unique group of people to do his bidding, and especially when it came to dealing with that constant thorn in his side - Israel. I believe he has already found that particular group of people to lead the charge against his rival in the end days. From among that sea of people will arise the Beast!

Before their identity is revealed, I wish to once again consider some of the crucial points that have been made in previous chapters. It is fundamentally important to maintain that there is only one Good Seed and to understand what that encompasses - the Word of God, Israel, etc. It is equally important to understand that there is one other seed diametrically opposed to the Good Seed. The serpent's seed is the serpent's word, which is specifically lies mingled with a measure of truth. In other words, any "holy book" other than the Word of God is a different seed, and by definition that means it is *zunim*, tares, and fathered by the serpent. That seed is embraced and disseminated by his followers who will ultimately rise up and strike at the "sons of the kingdom," Israel.

That these two seeds cannot coexist is evidenced by the respective fruit they produce. Bad fruit cannot grow from a good tree, because there is a mutual hostility between them. As a consequence, the bad seed desires to destroy the Good Seed. We see this throughout history in the likes of Pharaoh, Herod the Great, Esau, and most notably Nebuchadnezzar. Actually, we see this begin to take shape in the very beginning, just after God prophesied to the serpent of his demise and cursed him (Gen. 3:14 - 15). Notice that the serpent is the first *beast* (Gen. 3:1) to be cursed of God. Soon after this curse, the enmity between the two opposing seeds begins to develop with the birth of Cain and his brother Abel (Gen. 4). In fact, let us go back to the beginning once more and take a look at something that has remained unmentioned until now.

THE CURSE OF CAIN

> *"And He said, 'What have you done? The voice of your brother's blood cries out to Me from the ground. So now you are cursed from the earth, which has opened its mouth to receive your brother's blood from you hand. When you till the ground, it shall no longer yield its strength to you. A fugitive and a vagabond you shall be on the earth."*
>
> *- Genesis 4:10 -12*

Recall that earlier we raised the notion that, because the earth was cursed, the fruits of the earth were cursed also. If that is logical then is it not also logical to argue that, because the serpent was cursed (Gen. 3:14), his seed - that which proceeds from him - is cursed as well? Cain was cursed by God because he had, in effect, cursed what God had blessed, his brother Abel. Remember what God told Abraham.

"I will bless those who bless you, and I will curse him who curses you." - Genesis 12:3

I have not overlooked the fact that the LORD was speaking to Abraham centuries after the death of Abel. Nor has it escaped my attention that God was speaking of Abraham's seed. Yet, is not Abraham's seed those who are of faith? Was not Abel doing the works of Abraham even before Abraham was? Was it not faith that provoked him to acknowledge the need for a redeemer? I suggest to you that, by accepting his sacrifices, God blessed Abel. Why did Cain kill Abel? He was jealous of Abel's blessing, so Cain cursed his brother in perhaps the worst possible way - he butchered him. As a result, Cain himself was cursed. This is wholly sensible when you consider that, after all, Cain was of the "wicked one" (1 Jn. 3:12).

Now, let us look at the specifics of that curse, for I believe that the details will teach us the characteristics of the serpent's seed. In other words, what Cain initiates and the traits he exhibits will follow through into his descendants and *all* those who adamantly and blatantly emulate and express the nature of the serpent's wicked seed. It is also my opinion that when God placed a mark upon Cain, there may have been a reason in addition to the one given.

"And the LORD set a mark upon Cain, lest anyone finding him should kill him." - Genesis 4:15

Many writers, ancient and modern, have speculated as to what this mark was. The Talmud considered it to be the Hebrew נ *tav*, which in ancient form resembles the X. Others considered it to be a horn, or a physical malady. I personally believe that God stigmatized him physically so that others would know what he had done. Perhaps more importantly, he was marked so that those living in the end of days would pay attention. Why would He do that? Because God reveals the end from the beginning. Remember that this sequence of events began in Genesis 4:3 - "And in the process of time it came to pass. . . " That phrase in Hebrew is, ויהי מקץ ימים *Va'y'hi miketz yamim*, which literally is, "And it came to pass in the *end of days*."

The Hebrew word translated as "mark" is את *ote*. According to *Strong's Hebrew and Greek Definitions* it means, "a signal, beacon, monument, evidence, a sign." *Brown-Driver-Briggs Hebrew Definitions* adds that it also means "remembrance, a warning." It seems to me, ladies and gentlemen, that Cain is marked for *our* benefit. It is as if God is speaking from the beginning of time and saying, "Pay close attention to Cain and his descendants, for they signal what to be looking for in the end of days." You see, the seed of the serpent in the end will bear the mark of Cain.

It is important to remind the reader here of another foundational principle I introduced at the outset of this publication: there are eternal truths that have been concealed within Scripture until it is time for them to be revealed. I believe that is what we are dealing with here. Some of these truths can be hinted at through the Hebrew language itself (i.e. *pardes*: *peshat, remez, d'rush* and *sod*). Interestingly enough, Cain may even hint at this fact when he says:

"I shall be hidden from your face." - Genesis 4:14

The word that is translated as "hidden" is אסתר *esater*. The root of this word, סתר *satar*, means "concealed" or "secret" but in this way - being "concealed" with the object of being found. Imagine a fugitive running from a pursuer. The fugitive knows that sooner or later the pursuer will overtake him, so he decides to hide in the shadows and wait for the pursuer. When the pursuer comes into view, the coiled fugitive leaps from the shadows and strikes at the pursuer - *much like a serpent would do.*

Notice that when the LORD was sentencing Cain, He never said anything about Cain being hidden. It was Cain who made this startling declaration! Actually, the Hebrew phrasing could be rendered, "From your face I shall be hiding myself." This suggests that Cain decided to hide himself from God and, because the phrase is written in the imperfect tense, this concealment is considered to be ongoing. In other words, it is not yet finished - *Cain is still trying to hide!*

Knowing that someone would be looking for him, Cain decided to conceal himself and exist by lurking in the shadows. Only those who could find him would be able to kill him (Gen. 4:14) but what about those who could not detect him? I am suggesting that Cain was, in essence, telling God, "I am going to hide from You so that You will never find me, and I am prepared to strike against anyone who tries to reveal me." Does that sound like repentance? According to Cain, he would be "concealed" - until?

Does Cain, his life and his descendants have something to reveal to us relevant to our times. If so, was it all concealed until a future time? The Messiah said that there is nothing that has been kept secret that would not be revealed (Mk. 4:22). If Cain's story does

contain crucial information for this last-day generation, then the Holy Spirit will reveal this to us. What
Cain and the serpent attempted to hide will be found
in the Word. Just look for the mark.

THE FIRST ANTICHRIST?

Remember that when Cain ignored the need
for a redeemer, he was effectively denying the blood
of the Lamb. Cain is the first to embody the spirit of
"antichrist." Even when God rebuffed him for his neg-
lect and counseled him to do what was right, he still
refused. His failure turned him into a liar, a murderer,
and a nomad cursed to wander all the rest of his days.
In fact, he was the *first* liar. When God asked him the
whereabouts of his brother, he lied. He was the *first*
murderer and also the *first* robber in that he "took" his
brother's life, but not only that; he robbed his brother's seed from the earth. Actually, Cain emulated all of
the diabolical attributes his "father" the serpent gave
birth to. Satan is a liar and a murderer (Jn. 8:44) and a
robber (Jn. 10:1).

Like his "father," Cain was cursed by God. One
of the consequences of that curse was that no longer
could he till the ground with any success. The earth,
having reluctantly received the blood of Abel, rejected
Cain's efforts at producing its fruits. Furthermore, he
would have to wander the earth, never staying in one
place for too long. The Septuagint suggests that, as a
vagabond, Cain would be "groaning and trembling
upon the earth," and the horror of his crime would
haunt him forever.

It followed him eastward into a place of isola-
tion and banishment the Bible calls *Nod* or "wander-

ing." There he built a city - *a permanent dwelling* - in open defiance of his sentence to wander. It was as if he were saying to God, "I'll show you." If this is so, then Cain was not repentant. The mark he bore was not to protect a remorseful sinner, but it was to identify him as a liar, a murderer and a rebel determined to resist God and his purposes. Perhaps this was the reason God did not wish him to be immediately struck down, lest the world be unable to rightly determine the outcome of rebellion and discern the fruit of the wicked seed. When Cain built his city, its foundation initiated the heretical and rebellious kingdoms of the world. The spirit of the beast, no doubt, took up residence.

I am apparently not the only one who sees it this way. Note what Josephus and others have to say about Cain's spiritual disposition.

> *"And when Cain had traveled over many countries, he . . . built a city named Nod. . . . However, he did not accept of his punishment in order to amendment, but to increase his wickedness. . . . He augmented his household substance with much wealth, by rapine and violence. He excited his acquaintance to procure pleasures and spoils by robbery, and became a great leader of men into wicked courses. . . he changed the world into **cunning craftiness**."*
> - Antiquities of the Jews, Book 1, Chap. 2, Sect. 2

> *"Thus the original rebel against God was Cain. . . . He was, therefore, the original "Beast" who thought to change times and laws."*
> - William Dankenbring, "The Mark of Cain"

Cain's perverse and violent nature as well as

his disdain for the Righteous Seed apparently filtered down to his descendants. According to Josephus:

> "It came to pass that the posterity of Cain became exceeding wicked, every one . . . more wicked than the former. They were intolerable in war, and vehement in robberies; and if any one were slow to murder people, yet was he bold in his profligate behavior, in acting unjustly, and doing injuries for gain."
> - Antiquities, Book 1, Chap. 2, Sect. 2

Author Alfred Edersheim adds that:

> "It is very remarkable that we perceive in the Cainite race those very things which afterwards formed the characteristics of heathenism, as we find it among the most advanced nations of antiquity, such as Greece and Rome."
> - Old Testament History, p. 31

Some writings even credit Cain and his seed with being the originators of pagan worship, specifically mother-son worship and identify Cain as the original "sun god" and his wife as the first "Queen of Heaven." It is fascinating to consider.

The Scripture documents that one of his many grandsons, Lamech (not to be confused with the father of Noah), was the first man on record to take multiple wives (Gen. 4:19). In other words, it seems that Cain's seed introduced polygamy into the world in direct opposition to God's ideal of one man and one woman becoming one flesh (Gen. 2:24).

By his second wife, Lamech sired a son who was called Tubal-Cain, apparently a namesake of his infamous ancestor. Earlier we discussed what Cain means - "to acquire." "Tubal" is primarily translated as "proceeding forth from" or "issue." Thus תובל קין Tubal-Cain is understood to mean "to issue or proceed from Cain." This particular descendant then is Cain's seed personified. The word that תובל Tubal (also pronounced Tuval) comes from - תבל tevel - suggests an incestuous *mixture* of relatives or even species, i.e. bestiality. That, ladies and gentlemen, is an extremely interesting point in light of previous observations.

Another intriguing aspect of this man's brief appearance in Scripture is his vocation. Tubal-Cain was an artisan, whose particular craft is of great interest to our study, for he was the world's first smith.

> "And as for Zillah, she also bore Tubal-Cain, an instructor of every craftsman in bronze and iron."
> - Genesis 4:22

What kind of items did he make? Whatever they were they would have been comprised of bronze (brass) and iron and would have been something the world had never seen. That seems to cancel out farming tools. The world had already been introduced to farming decades earlier and presumably had already utilized certain tools to help them in this endeavor. Besides, what would a cursed people do with tools they couldn't use? The ground wouldn't produce anything for them. No, it seems that Tubal-Cain introduced to the world something far more revolutionary. In fact, tradition teaches that he made weapons of brass and iron.

One translation renders the above passage of Scripture as saying, "Tubal-Cain, hammering all kinds of cutting things in brass and iron." The First Century historian, Josephus, said that Tubal-Cain had great strength in military affairs, and that he taught men the way of melting metals and making armor. Some sources even say that Tubal-Cain means "scion of son of the lance" - the "son of the lance" being Cain. This meaning implies that Tubal-Cain simply improved on what his ancestor had started - taking something meant for good (in the case of Cain, a farming tool) and turning it into a weapon of war and terror.

It is supposed by some that the Romans took the name Tubal-Cain and transformed it into *Vulcan* by omitting *Tu* and using the "v" sound (which is accurate in Hebrew). Thus *Vul-Cain* became *Vulcan*. Vulcan is the Roman god of fire (Volcano) and is said to be the smithgod, maker of weapons. His Greek counterpart, Hephaestus, is said to have created a woman from clay and called her Pandora. Pandora, in turn, opened a supernatural jar and released the evils of the world upon mankind. Interestingly enough, the Bible says that Tubal-Cain had a sister, Naamah. Tradition states that Tubal-Cain had an incestuous relationship with her, creating confusion and multiplying wickedness upon the earth. Later on, it was with some of the descendants from this unnatural union that the "sons of God" began to mingle themselves (Gen. 6:2). Of course, as I have already pointed out, this distasteful action provoked the Deluge.

There is one other provocative element to Tubal-Cain's contribution to human history. The Bible says that he was an instructor of every craftsman in bronze and iron. The Hebrew word translated as "bronze," or "brass" in some cases, is נחשת *n'choshet*. It comes from the root word, נחש *nachash*, which can mean an "enchantment" or "incantation." It also means, "to hiss," but is most often translated as "serpent." In fact, the word used for serpent in Genesis 3 is that very word, נחש *nachash*. Therefore, Tubal-Cain was actually manufacturing the serpent's weapons. These were weapons the world had never seen before. You might even say this was the first appearance of WMDs - weapons of mass destruction. Why would a cursed race be making the serpent's weapons? It seems obvious to me - to crush the head of the Righteous Seed. Thankfully, the LORD says:

> *"Behold, I have created the blacksmith who blows the coals in the fire, who brings forth an instrument for his work; and I have created the spoiler to destroy. No weapon formed against you shall prosper. . . . This is the heritage of the servants of the LORD." - Isaiah 54:16-17*

Now that we have thoroughly covered the curse God placed on Cain, its ramifications and even the discreet clues contained in his lineage, I wish to return to the question we asked at the beginning of the chapter. Can we discern who the Adversary is using as his primary weapon against the Good Seed, Israel, in these last days? Based on what we have learned we need to look for those who:

* *Embrace a different "holy book" or seed.*
* *Display fruit at enmity with the fruit of the Word.*
* *Exhibit open hostility toward Israel.*
* *Ascribe to the Babylonian agenda, which includes: Conquering Jerusalem and subjugating the Jews.*
* *Are a mixed or mingled people.*

Furthermore, we should be able to observe in

them the same characteristics we see in Cain. Why? Because Cain is the seed of the serpent in the beginning, and God reveals the end from the beginning. Cain was, at least in my opinion, marked so that we might take note of him. Therefore in the end the serpent's seed should be noted for being:

* Murderers
* Robbers
* Polygamists
* Cursed
* Liars
* Nomads and Vagabonds
* Warriors (WMDs)
* Marked

There is one last thing to note. Though this may sound ridiculous, this group of people will not be noted for their farming skills, because God told Cain, and consequently his seed - the serpent's seed - that the ground would no longer yield her fruit for them. Why? Because Cain took a farming tool and bludgeoned his righteous brother to death, drenching the ground with his blood. So, after considering all of these characteristics, is there any group presently in the world that fits the bill? Keep in mind we are looking for a group that exhibits *all*, not just a few, of these characteristics. From this point on, those who tend to be politically correct should stop reading.

ARABIAN NIGHT

At the close of the previous chapter, it was revealed that the Hebrew word translated as "mingled" or "mixed" is מערב *m'arav*, and comes from the root word ערב *arav* or *arab*. This is no play on words. It is actually the same word by which we refer to those who come from the Arabian Peninsula. In fact, מערב

m'arav could be translated as "from Arabia." In other words, from a Hebraic perspective, to be Arab is to be mingled - mingled seed, if you will. Modern DNA research confirms that Arabs do not belong to a single "race."

As a Biblical term, *arav* is used to describe something that is "mingled." The aspect of being "mingled" stems from the impression one gets at twilight. As the sun begins to set, darkness begins to *mix* with light, night begins to *mingle* with day. Thus ערב *arav* is also rendered ערב *erev* or "evening." Furthermore, because this "mingling" occurs in the western skies, ערב *arav* is also a term used in the Bible to denote "Land of the Setting Sun," "west" or "westward" (Arabia being west of Babylonia). Consequently, westward movement from a biblical point of view is intended to imply "moving away" from God's laws and standards. Generally speaking, ערב *arav* is a derogatory term.

In some passages of the Bible, the term *arav* is used to designate "desert," or "people of the desert," or a "NOMAD." Contrary to the Arab belief that other semitic peoples emigrated *from* Arabia to other regions of the Levant, the people of Arabia have been ethnically traced to different groups whose homelands are *outside* of the Peninsula. In other words, their forebears ventured *into* Arabia from other regions - they were wanderers. Biblically speaking, to be Arab is to be both a nomad and to be from mingled seed. That, ladies and gentlemen is interesting indeed.

Some may read this and think, "What about America? All of our ancestors wandered into this continent from other lands. We are a nation of mingled people, a melting pot in fact." This is all true, however, with all of our faults have we been able to get the ground to render its fruits? Yes! Are we a nation of polygamists? No! Has this nation historically shown an outward and violent antagonism toward Israel? No! Have we historically rejected God's Word and the Lamb? Now consider the Arab culture (not necessarily the people) and ask yourself these same questions.

Most Arabs consider themselves to be descendants of Ishmael through his twelve sons. Ishmael, of course, was the offspring of Abraham and the Egyptian Hagar. There are other tribes who constitute Arab ancestry including the Midianites, the Sabeans and a group the Scriptures refer to as Kenites. In Hebrew they are called הקיני ha'Keini. Oddly enough, the root of this word is the name קין Cain! The point is this: the Hebrew language and history itself confirms that Arabs are a mingled race of people whose ancestors were wanderers. Those ancestors were also traditional and familial antagonists of God's People, Israel.

With regard to the family ties between Arab and Hebrew, it seems noteworthy to mention that the word ערב arav is very similar to the word עבר avar. As far as the spelling of these words go, they are identical except for the fact that two letters are reversed. We have elaborated on the meaning arav and we know that it identifies the Arab people. The other word, avar, can mean "to impregnate," or when used as a noun it forms the word for "embryo." This word then hints of life, seed and the fruit. The most common use of this root means "to cross over." It is an agricultural term used to signify those who cross over from land that does not produce fruit into a land that does. From this root word, we get עברי ivri or "Hebrew" as in "He is a Hebrew."

עבר
avar "Hebrew"

ערב
arav "Arab"

The first עברי *Ivri* or Hebrew was Abraham, because he *crossed over* the Jordan River from a land of idolaters into a land where God would establish His name. This is the land that God promised to Abraham and to his seed - the seed of promise - forever! While in this land, he and his wife decided that to have an heir meant that he should go into his wife's Egyptian handmaid. The result of that decision led to Ishmael, which led to his twelve sons, which led to a large segment of the Arab people. I suggest that in a manner of speaking, tares were seeded among the wheat. As politically incorrect and insensitive as this may sound, "mingling" (*arav*), and by extension a race antagonistic to Israel was not God's plan. Does that mean God does not love Arab people? Not at all. In fact, He has and will receive *any* man who calls upon the name of the LORD. Still, it is necessary to face the reality of what the Biblical record reveals. What we understand *Arav* to be came as the result of failing to receive God's Word. Therefore, those who sprout (I speak in spiritual terms) from *arav* - "mingled" - are not the promised seed of Abraham. They are not the Good Seed.

If you look closely at the two words - ערב *arav* and עבר *avar* - they look *almost* identical, but they are not. It is, in fact, that small, seemingly insignificant distinction that makes all the difference in the world. It changes everything. It is like the wheat and the tare: to the untrained eye they look almost identical as well, but they are not. One is sown by the owner of the field and produces the desired fruit, while the other is sown by the Adversary and produces a degenerate fruit, which is, I might add, in constant conflict with the wheat. It struggles for the same sunlight, the same rain, and the same ground!

Isn't it interesting that the source of all the contention in the Middle East, the war on Terror, etc., is the very *ground* that God promised to Abraham and his righteous seed? Is it mere coincidence that these two aforementioned Hebrew words are formed by the same letters but are simply arranged a little differently? Is God trying to tell us something through the Hebrew language itself? It is as if the DNA of these two words (seeds), which seem to be so similar is, nevertheless, arranged differently. When looking at the "seed," the differences seem ever-so-slight, but by the time the fruit appears, the distinctions are drastic. You see, these two seeds produce offspring that hate one another. One or the other must give ground to the superior force in climactic battle - that time is here! The sun is starting to set, darkness is beginning to mingle with light, night is falling. Therefore, we must:

"work the works of Him who sent me while it is day; the night is coming when no one can work." - Jn. 9:4

EXAMINING THE FRUIT

Before I go any further, I think it is necessary to clarify something for the reader. To consider *arav* a derogatory term is not intended to mean that all Arabs are evil people. I am not, and the Bible is certainly not racist. In fact, one of the points I have labored so strenuously to make is that, as far as God is concerned, justification or judgment has never been determined by genealogies. It has always been a matter of faith or the lack thereof. That God used the Hebrew culture to disseminate His Seed to other cultures does not guarantee that those who are born of that culture or those who assimilate into that culture are necessarily "good seed." As I have noted multiple times, to be regarded as Israel is dependent on whether you receive and reproduce the Good Seed.

Likewise, just because it seems that the Adversary has used the Arab culture, not to mention other cultures including our own, to disseminate his seed to the world does not mean that everyone reared in one of these cultures is wicked. To the contrary, anyone - whether Arab, Jew, Hispanic, Asian or Christian - who calls upon the name of the LORD is born again as "good seed" because of the Good Seed. That being said, it is still true that God and the Adversary have used flesh and blood to propagate their respective agendas.

Consider עבר *avar* (i.e. Hebrew) as being synonymous with the Good Seed, Torah - the Word of God. From this seed the biblically Hebrew culture was born. To be assigned to this "culture" is to be designated as one who is identified as Israel regardless of natural ethnicity. This "culture" enjoys a land flowing with milk and honey. Its inhabitants "crossed over" in order to produce the good fruit in abundance. According to the Apostle Paul, the fruit produced by this "culture" is personified by:

"Love, joy, peace, longsuffering, gentleness, goodness, faith, meekness and temperance."
- Galatians 5:22-23

On the other hand ערב *arav* (i.e. Arab) is synonymous with another "culture," another word - another seed - called the *Qur'an*. The "faith" it espouses, Islam, was born in the Arabian peninsula and was spawned by the Arab culture itself. To be categorized with this "culture" whether ethnically Arab or not is to be considered "mingled" and "nomadic." Consequently, the ground this "culture" inhabits will not produce the fruit the other enjoys. In a literal sense, topsoil does not exist in Arabia for the most part. Centuries of extreme heat and cold, in conjunction with intense windstorms, have condemned the region to barren nothingness. What vegetation does grow is due primarily to modern fertilization and irrigation, producing some of the costliest produce in the world. The ground simply will not produce fruit!

Still, just as the Torah produces "fruit after its kind," the *Qur'an* reproduces itself through its own respective fruit. This is odd if you bear in mind that both cultures claim to call upon the same God. Both claim the same spiritual father, Abraham. Considering who gave birth to these two cultures, it would *seem* they are brothers. But the question must be asked - "Do they produce the same fruit?" If the answer is "No," then we must conclude that the seed is not the same. If they are of differing seeds, then only one can come from the Good Seed - the other *must* be the serpent's seed. Now it is time to compare the nature of these two "seeds" by examining their fruit. I will assume that the reader is familiar with the Fruit of the Spirit so that Islam's fruit can be emphasized.

> *"War, not friendship is mandatory until Islam reigns everywhere." (Sura 8:39, 2:193)*

This quote from the Islamic "holy book," the *Qur'an*, helps us to understand something that has been accepted in Islam for centuries. Muhammad's most enduring legacy is that there are only two lands - the land of peace (*Dar al-Islam*) and the land of war (*Dar al-Harb*). The Islamic objective is to make the world one under the teachings of the *Qur'an* and the Arab culture. Early on, to be identified with Islam was to be connected with Arabia and its culture to such an extent that a convert would be bound to associate with one of the Arab tribes and to take a new Arab name. In short, it meant removing all traces of the past and becoming *Arab* - "mingled."

Holy war, or *Jihad*, was and is the methodology employed to expand *Dar al-Islam*, to further the influence of the Arab culture, and to establish the kingdom of *Allah* on earth. Then and now, this method translates into this: people must perish by Islam's sword. The will to kill and murder in the name of *Allah* seems to be an acceptable attribute of a faithful Muslim.

"It is not for any Prophet to have captives until he hath made slaughter in the land." - Sura 8:68

Other Islamic writings suggest that killing Jews and Christians is *especially* acceptable if not altogether mandatory. Muhammad exposes his enmity of the Jews in the *Qur'an* and suggests that even stone walls will speak out and aid Muslims in the war against Israel.

"O Muslim! There is a Jew hiding behind me, so kill him. . . . We have put enmity and hatred amongst them till the Day of Resurrection. (Sura 5:60, 64)

In his book, *The Sword of the Prophet*, author Serge Trifkovic infers that this will to murder is actually an inherent trait of the Arab culture. He says:

"Robbery and murder outside the protective confines of one's clan were not deemed bad per se, they were judged by the results as a means to an end. The respect of one's neighbor was strictly contingent on his power and his means." - *The Sword of the Prophet*, p. 17

To some, this type of accusation would seem overtly biased and racist. Yet, here are the facts. In the last twenty years, over two million people have died in conflicts involving Muslim communities. Why? It is a fact that Muslims carry out many, if not the majority of the worst acts of terrorism. Tell the truth. When you think of a terrorist, what image pops into your mind? Do you typically think of the Timothy McVeighs of the world, or do you conjure images of people like Muhammad Atta and Usama bin Ladin?

A DIFFERENT SEED

Now that we have briefly compared the fruit of Islam with that of our own faith, let us now evaluate the difference between the two seeds themselves - the Torah and the *Qur'an*. From Islam's point of view, the Bible is a distorted and tainted "book." As far as Muhammad is concerned, the Torah is a "barbarous Qur'an" and stands opposed to the true Arabic one (Sura 41:44). The "true" Arabic *Qur'an* places Ishmael, not Isaac, upon an altar atop Mt. Moriah. From my point of view, this is an example of taking a small measure of truth and mingling it with a lie.

Despite the claims of both Christians and Muslims that *Allah* and the God of the Bible are one and the same, the *Qur'an* dogmatically states that:

"Allah begets not and was not begotten, that is, he is no Son; and no one is like him, which means he is no Holy Spirit" - Sura 112

Furthermore the *Qur'an* argues that "Isa," who we refer to as Y'shua (Jesus) is not the Son of Allah, only a special prophet. Islam also claims that Y'shua was not crucified. Instead they insist that God confused the Jews and consequently, they crucified someone else. Furthermore, it is taught that in the last days Isa will return to tell the world that he lied and that he is not the Son of God. The dilemma these statements create is this: either God is schizophrenic, the *Qur'an* is a lie or the Bible is a lie. The Scripture says:

"Who is a liar but he who denies that Y'shua is the Messiah? He is antichrist who denies the Father and the Son." - 1 John 2:22

It now becomes obvious what we are dealing with here. We are not discussing a simple difference of opinion, or a different way to pray; it is not even about a different path to the same goal. The issue at hand is a fundamental question that goes all the way back to the beginning of time - "Is man in need of a redeemer?" To deny that he is, is to deny that Y'shua is the Messiah and God made flesh. To espouse such doctrine is, by definition, the spirit of antichrist.

Nevertheless, this is what Islam maintains.

Islam flatly rejects what the Messiah accomplished through His death. According to their doctrine, for a Muslim to obtain their conception of salvation means that one's entire life must be spent striving to obtain God's favor. If Allah wills, that individual will be rewarded in heaven for his good deeds. If Allah doesn't will it - *que sera sera* - for the *Qur'an* also says that Allah "forgives whom he will, and he chastises whom he will" (Sura 5:18)! In short, and this is the point, Islam denies the need for the blood of the Lamb. This is *exactly* what Cain was guilty of, which led to the murder of his righteous brother Abel! That they share the same contempt for the Redeemer, in my opinion, also explains why some Muslims share in Cain's murderous nature.

The most alarming aspect of this dilemma is that true Muslims, those who believe in the fundamentals of Islam, really believe they are right and we are wrong, just as certainly as all true believers in Messiah believe that we have received the one Good Seed. Therein lies the conflict. However, this conflict cannot be limited to debates on television or in newspaper editorials. This conflict, according to Scripture, is destined to engulf the entire world. Why? For the answer I again refer to Mr. Trifkovic.

> "The problem of Islam, and the rest of the world with Islam, is not the remarkable career of Muhammad per se. . . . It is the religion's claim that the words and acts of its prophet provide the universally valid standard of morality as such, for all time and all men." - Sword of the Prophet, p. 53

In other words, Mr. Trifkovic infers that,

because they believe the *Qur'an* is the inerrant word of God, and because the *Qur'an* urges them forward in the battle against the infidels, they will never rest until Islam is universal. It is the word of Allah, this other seed, that provokes them to action. This aggressive nature is merely a reflection of this seed and of Allah.

Long before Muhammad was born, the tribes of Arabia worshiped over three hundred different deities at the *Ka'aba* in Mecca. The most dominant of these deities was the moon god, *Hubal*. This particular name was used less than others, but is the one that corresponds to the BABYLONIAN *ba'al* or *bel* - the chief among all gods. Again, there were several variations of *Hubal*, whose title was *al'ilah* - shortened by frequency of usage to *allah*. This means that *allah* was the name of a *deity* long before Muhammad was born, and it also explains why Islam's emblem is the crescent moon - *allah* is actually the moon god.

Muhammad and his peers were certainly familiar with this pagan deity. In fact, Muhammad's particular tribe revered *allah* as the superior of all other deities worshiped in the *Ka'aba*. It would seem then, that during his ascent to power Muhammad merely incorporated *allah* into his new "revelation." According to some sources, even though Muhammad preached of one god, he nevertheless referred to all of the idols in the *Ka'aba* as "allah," in effect merging them all into one and calling them by the same name.

Now ask yourself a few questions. Why would the *one* God give mankind *two* different and contradictory "revelations"? Why would the God of the Universe allow Himself to be likened to one of the heavenly luminaries He created, and the lesser one at that? Would the God of the Bible share His glory and

His name with idols made of wood and stone?

"I am the LORD, that is My name: and My glory I will not give to another, nor My praise to carved images." - Isaiah 42:8

Despite what a lot of theologians and Muslim public relations people have to say, Allah is absolutely *not* the same as the God of Abraham, Isaac and Jacob. Consequently, whatever Allah says should be considered as unreliable. If Allah says something that contradicts what God said, by definition, that makes Allah's word another seed - the seed of the serpent. For centuries this seed has been among a select group of people who have, in turn, reproduced this degenerate seed through the fruit of that seed - lies, murder, fear, intimidation and terror. Lately, however, the desert winds have carried that seed around the world. The seed has germinated, and now the world is faced with what Y'shua called:

"The days of vengeance, that all things which are written may be fulfilled." - Luke 21:22

THE WAR ON TERROR

"I will instill terror into the hearts of the unbelievers, smite ye about their necks and smite all their finger tips of them." - Sura 8:12

The *Qur'an* makes it clear that Allah "does not love the unbelievers" (Sura 3:32). In Islam's eyes, anyone who does not accept the *Qur'an* as the word of Allah and Muhammad as his prophet is an infidel.

Based on what the world has lived through in the past few years, and upon how the *Qur'an* regards the unbeliever, some Muslims probably consider that the "only good infidel is a dead infidel." Though I say that "tongue-in-cheek" the reality is that this sentiment is the very reason the world is facing global terrorism.

It is very obvious that Muhammad was keen on ridding the world of undesirables. Moreover, it seems that Muhammad was particularly fond of beheading as a method of execution for all infidels. On one occasion, when the severed head of a nemesis was cast in front of him, the *timid, peaceful* Muhammad exclaimed that the offering surpassed that of the "choicest camel in Arabia." Well, after all, Allah said to, "smite them about their necks." It appears that the anti-Messiah will share this obsession with beheading and will take the words of the *Qur'an* to heart. John the Revelator records that:

> "I saw the souls of those who had been beheaded for their witness to Y'shua and for the word of God, who had not worshiped the beast or his image, and had not received his mark on their foreheads or on their hands." - Revelation 20:4

Is this simply a coincidence or an indication that what is being put forth in this book is not so far-fetched? The world is just now beginning to deal with a problem that has been simmering for centuries. Islam feels it is their destiny to rule the world. The problem is that most politicians and governments, our own not excluded, do not understand the spiritual aspect of this current war on terror. It seems that many feel this is just a limited conflict against a handful of thugs. To the contrary, this is an ages-old war that is on the brink of coming to a head. Militant, fundamental Islam is flexing its muscle and will soon try to enforce their world view on every one else. Those who resist will do so at their own peril. My main problem with this likelihood? In their eyes, I am an infidel!

It appears to me that the fundamentals of Islam dictate to those who would be deemed fundamentalists that the world cannot continue to exist dominated by "crusaders" or Christians. Usama bin Ladin agrees with me. That is why he is at the epicenter of this conflict. He and thousands, perhaps tens-of-thousands, of his fellow Muslims have been spreading out through the world in anticipation of a final and decisive *jihad* - one that would establish Islamic rule over all nations. The last time Muslims generated this degree of empirical fervor, Europe came alarmingly close to becoming a Muslim continent. That was over 500 years ago, so the man on the street has not given radical Islam a second thought - not until September 11, 2001, that is.

Since then people have begun to take a closer look at this religion. Some have come away thinking that Muslims, for the most part, are law-abiding peaceful people. I would agree that many, if not most Muslims, are peace-loving people who strive for nothing more than to make a living and take care of their family. However, I would also point out that these Muslims, like the majority of those who consider themselves Christians, do not know the fundamentals of their own faith. They do no know what their holy book says, but only what they are told it says. To put it bluntly, Usama bin Ladin is a good Muslim in that he is faithful to the teachings of the prophet Muhammad. He also exhibits the fruit of his "father."

That being said, let us ponder a few points. Based on what the Scripture reveals about Babylon, its relationship to the serpent and its antagonism for God and for His people, should the fact that the War on Terror has led us to, of all places, ancient Babylonia on a search for WMDs be relegated as coincidental? Is it also coincidental that this war began as the result of an attack by people whose "faith" was born in ערב Arabia? By the way, most of the hijackers hailed from Saudi Arabia, which is considered to be the most extremist of all the Muslim states. That is pretty frightening when you consider that Saudi Arabia is lauded as one of the United States' best allies in the region.

Should I ignore the fact that Islam's loftiest aspirations involve destroying Israel and anyone aligning themselves in any way with Israel? From the Bible's point of view those who hold to this unholy tenet are classified as "cursed." Are not those who pursue this "ambition" following in the way of Cain? Should I overlook the other centuries-old characteristics exhibited by Islam and the nomadic culture that spawned it - characteristics that just happen to mirror those of the world's first nomad? Can I ignore the lies, the murder, the robbery?

Am I to shrug off the fact that many in the Muslim world emulate the polygamy that Cain's seed first introduced to the world? Ought the oil beneath the sand override the fact that the land from which Islam sprouted is nothing more than a barren wasteland, incapable of producing anything else? Is this all happenstance?

Are you aware that Islam has eschatological expectations? They believe that their "messiah" is coming. In Islamic commentary (hadith), he is referred to as the "coming guided one" - *al mahdi*. It is believed that he will come in the end of days, riding upon a white horse. He, with the aid of Isa (Jesus), will convert the world to Islam either by volition or by the sword. In the end, so the belief goes, the entire world will become *Dar al-Islam*, the land of peace - the kingdom of Allah. Many of the insurgents pouring into Iraq from neighboring Muslim countries believe that Iraq (Babylonia) is to be the springboard for this Islamic empire and that NOW is the time for the advent of *al-mahdi*, the Islamic messiah. Don't you find it interesting that their messianic hopes provoke them to seek out Jews and Christians for hostages and execute them by cutting off their heads while screaming, "*Allahu akhbar*"?

This messianic fervor manifested itself in another way just after Saddam's overthrow. For decades, the Shi'ite majority in Iraq had been oppressed by the infamous despot. When U.S. forces removed Saddam in April 2002, that same month thousands of Shi'ites clogged the streets of Karbala, Iraq, to commemorate an ancient battle and the death of one of Shi'a Islam's esteemed *imams* - Hussein, son of Ali and Fatima (Fatima was Muhammad's favored daughter).

Tradition says that when Hussein, who saw himself as somewhat of a messianic figure, was killed, his death was seen as a martyrdom and in some way, furthered the belief that some day Islam's messiah would come. Tradition also teaches that the Hussein loyalists who survived the battle carved wounds into their forehead. As the blood flowed they chanted, "*Allahu akhbar*," signifying not only their loyalty to Hussein but to Allah. In effect, they were offering their life's blood to Allah, pledging to overcome all infidels.

In April 2002, U.S. soldiers who happened to be in Karbala when this bloody rite was reinstituted were told to "stand down" and give adequate space to the mob who was increasing in both numbers and violence with every passing minute. Pictures of the crowd showed agitated men and boys screaming, blood flowing from self-inflicted wounds, many resembling a large "X" in the middle of their forehead. From the photographs, there is no mistaking that their chants of "*allahu akhbar*" were directed directly at our military personnel. It is as if they were committing their life - their very soul - to Allah and the triumph of Islam over the *American* unbelievers.

There are those who would have us believe that when these men and boys scream "*Allahu akhbar*," or when these barbarians cut the heads off of defenseless victims and praise Allah with this chant, that they are declaring, "God is great!" That simply is not true. They are actually announcing, "Allah is *greater*." My question is, "Greater than who?" Are the followers of the moon-god proclaiming him to be greater than the Son? If so, then this is blasphemy. If true, then the mark they place in their foreheads by which they pledge their very souls to him is also blasphemy - a *mark* of blasphemy. So then, has the mark of Cain reappeared to identify the serpent's seed?

Ladies and gentlemen, I am convinced that all the evidence - that which was revealed in the beginning through Cain and his seed, and that which is contained in the writings of Daniel and all the other prophets - clearly points to the Islamic world as the sea of people from which the anti-Messiah shall arise. Somewhere in that chaotic cauldron, there exists another Cain, another Esau, another Nebuchadnezzar.

> *"And I saw a beast rising up out of the sea, having seven heads and ten horns, and on his horns ten crowns, and on his heads a blasphemous name."*
> - *Revelation 13:1*

I do not stand alone in this diagnosis. Many others have recently arrived at the same conclusion. I was somewhat excited to learn that the ancient Jewish commentator Ibn Ezra (1089-1164 C.E.) wholeheartedly believed that the last kingdom would be an Islamic one. In part, his conclusion was based on Daniel's usage of the word ערב *arav* to describe the feet with ten toes, iron *mingled* with clay. Apparently without knowing, I picked up on the same clue he had centuries before. It just goes to show you, there is nothing new under the sun.

There are other similar clues in the Hebrew text that, at the very least, hint at the identity of the end time kingdom. In my opinion they confirm the identity of the beast, and furthermore strongly imply that September 11th, and the subsequent War on Terror will set the stage for all of these things - the advent of the Beast and the Coming of the Son of Man - to come to pass. One of these clues is found - where else? - in the beginning.

> *"The earth was also corrupt before God, and the earth was filled with violence."* - *Genesis 6:11*

Earlier I addressed the issue of the "days of Noah" being likened to the days of the Messiah's coming. With that in mind, if something in the Hebrew text above hints at something that is unique to our day, should it be interpreted as God trying to reveal a truth that has heretofore gone unrecognized? While you ponder the question, I will tell you that this verse suggests that the tactics of radical Islam - terrorism - will pervade the entire earth. In fact, the Hebrew text mentions one of these terror organizations by name.

The group *Hamas* (The Islamic Resistance Movement) is based primarily in the Gaza Strip and the so-called West Bank. However, over the last few years Hamas has been expanding their theater of operations. For example, in December 2003, one Hamas-related operative was caught before he could cross into the U.S. from Canada and fulfill his mission to kill Jews in New York City. This is just one of many incidents of this nature. The implications are that Hamas, like al-Qaeda, is spreading out through the globe. The fascinating thing about this development is that the Bible may have already predicted this. The Hebrew word that is translated as "violence" in Genesis 6:11 is חמס *hamas*!

Anyone who has ever studied prophecy knows that Daniel 9 is required reading when it comes to understanding the last days. This chapter reveals details about Israel's fate, the anti-Messiah, and the seven-year Tribulation. Yet with all that is revealed on the surface of the text, perhaps the most startling revelation is found beneath the surface, hidden within the Hebrew language itself.

As the chapter begins, Daniel was reading the books of Jeremiah, specifically the prophecies concerning the captivity in Babylon. As he read it dawned on him WHY Judah was taken to Babylon.

*"O Lord, righteousness belongs to You, but to us shame of face . . . to the men of Judah, to the inhabitants of Jerusalem and **all** Israel, those near and those far off . . . because of the unfaithfulness which they have committed against You." - Daniel 9:7*

He continued to acknowledge that Israel's bondage was a direct consequence of the fact that Israel had continually failed to follow God's Torah and continued to disregard the warnings of His prophets. Then in Daniel 9:11 (notice 9-1-1) he says:

*"Yes, **all Israel** has transgressed Your law, and has departed so as not to obey Your voice; therefore the curse and the oath written in the Law of Moses the servant of God have been poured out on us, because we have sinned against Him." - Daniel 9:11*

Notice that Daniel states "all Israel" is guilty of transgressing the Torah. Let me also ask you to recall the biblical definition of "Israel." Therefore, I believe this statement pertains to the natural branches as well as the branches that have been grafted in - you and me! The ramifications are this: "the curse" for disobeying the Torah and breaking the covenant has been poured out upon *all* Israel, not just Jews. The Hebrew word translated as "curse" is אלה *alah*. In other words, *alah* is poured out because of our disobedience. Apparently, *alah* - THE CURSE - is to serve as a "rod of correction" for God's people. This would be consistent with the role of previous oppressors and anti-Messiah prototypes. God actually referred to Nebuchadnezzar as "my servant" (Jer. 25:9).

The name of the Islamic deity is, in Hebrew,

אללה *allah*. The spelling is slightly different, but the hint at the identity of the last prince to oppress Israel and consequently cause them to turn to their God is very strong. His very name is identified as a "curse," reminiscent of that first man to be cursed of God. Should the fact this is revealed in Daniel 9:11 be considered happenstance, or is God trying to tell us something?

Personally, I am convinced that He *is* trying to tell us something. I believe that He is bringing to light information - revelation - that would have made no sense to any other generation. That the global aspirations of militant Islam is surfacing just now is, in my opinion, no accident. It is, in fact, a satanic response to what God has determined to do within His body - to revive us so that we may accomplish what He has placed us here to do. In essence, it boils down to this: there are two groups - those who have been marked by God as "Righteous," and those who have been marked by God as being the successors to Cain - the serpent's seed.

$\mathcal{T}_{EN}$

DAYS OF ELIJAH

"For the testimony of Y'shua, is the spirit of prophecy."
- Revelation 19:10

In the months prior to the D-Day invasion of 1944, the Allies undertook a strategy to leak false information to the Nazis concerning the upcoming European campaign. They wanted the Nazis to think that the main invasion force would try to come ashore north of Normandy in Calais. Hitler took the bait and concentrated a large contingent of veteran forces in northern France. When the Allies began the offensive in Normandy, Hitler and the German High Command remained convinced that the coast of Calais was still to be the spearhead of the attack. By the time they realized that Normandy was the primary target it was too late. It would only be a matter of time before the entire European continent would be freed from the oppression of Hitler's rule.

Here is my point. The serpent is the most cunning of all the beasts of the field. Unless the Holy Spirit teaches and leads us, we are no match for his schemes. Taking his craftiness into consideration, is it possible that for centuries the serpent has been leaking false information - seeded with just enough truth to make it sound plausible - in order for believers to focus on one end-time scenario while the real threat grows elsewhere? In other words, while most students of Bible prophecy remain fixated on Rome for the emergence of the Beast, is it possible that the Bible points us toward Babylon?

Consider how a serpent acts. When a serpent is stalking prey, he doesn't attract attention to himself. He uses stealth and cunning to mark his victim. He hides in the shadows until it is time to strike. When he sinks his fangs in, the poison renders the victim unconscious until death comes. The prey is then devoured.

Likewise, the Adversary hides in the shadows, coaxing mankind into spiritual slumber until he has opportunity to inject his poisonous word rendering his prey incapable of discerning truth from lies. Is it possible that his methodology has affected how we view the end times? If so, and if we hope to awaken from the stupor, then we must re-examine the Sacred Text that God has provided for us. His Word, the Torah, not only teaches us how to live today, but what to anticipate tomorrow.

Though we are promised that the serpent and his devilish seed will not prevail, still, I have wondered why God allowed Cain to live. Why didn't He allow the earth to open and swallow him along with Abel's blood? I have also wondered why He allowed the tares to remain in the field alongside of the wheat, even though the crop and the field itself would be con-taminated. I have come to this conclusion. He wanted Cain to live in his punishment, just like the tares were permitted to grow with the wheat, allowing the fruit of rebellion to develop to its utmost. Why? So that in the end, all would see that sin and rebellion cannot produce what only the Good Seed can. Moreover, all could witness the effects of the curse that comes from rejecting the forgiveness wrought by acknowledging the need for the blood of the Redeemer.

We cannot forget that, from the beginning, the Promised Seed was destined to destroy the seed of the serpent. The serpent, in turn, sought to destroy Him and will pursue this course until the bitter end. We also cannot forget that the first man to oppose the Seed and the Blood of the Lamb was also the first man to be stigmatized with a mark that identified him as all that is unholy and blasphemous. In the end, the anti-Messiah will exhibit the same traits as Cain. Like Cain, he will epitomize the very nature of the serpent, and will be empowered to enforce the consequences of that nature upon all to the degree that mankind will be compelled to be stigmatized with his satanic and blasphemous mark or face death (Rev. 13:16-17).

Notwithstanding, the Bible promises that, in the end, the Righteous will be able to look down into the pit upon him who terrorized the world - the king of Babylon - and say:

> "Is this the man who made the earth tremble, who shook kingdoms, who made the world as a wilder-ness and destroyed its cities?" - Isaiah 14:16-17

That the man of sin is the king of Babylon, there is no mistaking. From the beginning, biblical evidence points to this region and to the dominant culture of that region as the Number One suspect. The king of Babylon will arise and try to bring the Muslim people together - "they will *mingle* with the seed of men" (Dan. 2:43) - and create a pan-Islamic political entity that will seek to control their own destiny as well as further the global interests of Islam. As a result, all nations and particularly Israel - *all Israel* - will be affected. Still it should be understood that our enemy is not the Arab people. The Arab or the Muslim or the Buddhist, or the Christian for that matter, who receives the one and only Good Seed, the Messiah Y'shua, is reborn as Israel. Paul plainly tells us that:

"We do not wrestle against flesh and blood, but against principalities, against powers, against the rulers of the darkness of this age, against spiritual hosts of wickedness in the heavenly places."
- *Ephesians 6:12*

Nevertheless, every spirit must have a body to operate through. The Holy Spirit works through the Body of Messiah and, yes, the Spirit of anti-Messiah works through his body. So the struggle continues. The wheat is pitted against the tare; the tare is attempting, one last time I believe, to choke out the wheat. Like their master. the tares will lurk in the shadows before striking the final time. In the face of hostility, however, we must hold on. We must continue to speak the truth, to defend the truth and, if need be, die for the truth. The Messiah promised that those who endure until the end, those shall be saved (Mt. 24:13). Those who give up their lives for His sake will rule and reign with Him (Rev. 20:4). Be encouraged - the wheat harvest is about to commence.

THE WHEAT AND THE CHAFF

"His winnowing fork is in His hand, and He will thoroughly clean out His threshing floor, and gather His wheat into the barn; but He will burn up the chaff with unquenchable fire." - Matthew 3:12

It must be understood that a particular element of the harvest directly and harshly affects the wheat. You see, the wheat - the fruit the Good Seed produces - must be threshed. As the wheat matures, a hard calloused casing grows in order to insulate the kernel of wheat. That outer shell - if you will, the "flesh" of the wheat - is not good for anything. It must be removed and so it is by striking the wheat against a hard surface. This "threshing" breaks off the hard unfruitful shell and exposes the precious kernel. When this process is completed, a mixture of wheat and chaff lies on the ground.

In Biblical days, the harvester would then take a winnowing fork and begin to sift the wheat by tossing the mixture into the air, usually during the breezy part of the day. The wind (Heb. רוח *ruach*, also translated as "spirit") would blow the lighter chaff away, leaving the heavier grains of wheat to fall to the ground. Ideally, when the sifting was complete, the harvester would have nothing left on the threshing floor but wheat, which would then be gathered and stored. In reality, he would be storing seed. In the end, the very thing that birthed the wheat is what is harvested from the wheat.

Thus, the end-time revival I referred to in the Introduction is, in reality, the sifting process needed to expose the wheat and rid the world of tares and chaff.

It is, in essence, a process designed to return us to where we came from and restore that which has been lost. The last day revival is a process intended to resuscitate that which is unconscious. How will we know when this revival has begun? The parable teaches that you know the harvest is near when the seed begins to put forth its fruit - not some other fruit - for all to see. In other words, when the sons of the Kingdom begin to *truly* reflect the Word of God - all of it - we can be sure the harvest is at hand.

REMEMBER MOSES

> *"Behold, I will send you Elijah the prophet before the coming of the great and dreadful day of the LORD. And he will turn the hearts of the fathers to the children, and the hearts of the children to their fathers, lest I come and strike the earth with a curse."*
> - Malachi 4:5-6

When asked by His disciples why Elijah must first come, Y'shua replied that, "Indeed, Elijah is coming first and will *restore all things*" (Mt. 17:11). He then told them that if they were willing to accept it, Elijah had already come, referring to John the Baptist (Mt. 17:12-13). He, of course, was the forerunner to the Messiah who came in "the spirit and power of Elijah" to "turn the hearts of the fathers to the children" (Lk. 1:17). In short, the Messiah reveals that the "Elijah" in Malachi's prophecy isn't *necessarily* "the Elijah" but can be that one (or those) who have the same spirit and calling. Other than the fact he was a Tishbite, we really don't know where Elijah came from. Some traditions believe that Elijah, one of the greater prophets, was actually a former Gentile who had come to faith in the God of Israel. If true, the prophetic implications are remarkable and make perfect sense in light of what is going on within the Body of Messiah.

"Elijah's" mission is to prepare the way of His Coming by turning "the hearts of the fathers to the children, and the hearts of the children to the fathers." This is not to be understood as addressing typical father-son relationships, at least it is not limited to that. It should be understood that "the fathers" are the patriarchs of faith, i.e. Abraham. We, as the children, have turned our hearts away from them (and what they taught). Elijah comes to rectify that error, thus "restoring all things." In other words, he (they) being called of God initiate the last day revival. How does "Elijah" accomplish this? The answer is found in Malachi's prophecy in the verses prior to the announcement about Elijah.

*"For behold, the day is coming, burning like an oven, and all the proud, yes, all who do wickedly will be stubble. And the day which is coming shall burn them up, says the LORD of hosts, that will leave them neither root nor branch. But to you who fear My name the Sun of Righteousness shall arise with healing in His wings . . .You shall **trample** the wicked, for they shall be ashes under the **soles** of your feet. On the day that I do this, says the LORD of hosts. **Remember the Law (torah) of Moses**, My servant, which I commanded him in Horeb for **all Israel**, with the statutes and judgments. Behold, I will send you Elijah the prophet. . ."*

- Malachi 4:1-5

I firmly believe that the days in which we live are, as the song declares, "the days of Elijah." The prophet's mission was to call the people back to where they had strayed from. The Baptist's mission was the same so that the way of the LORD might be prepared. Likewise today, "Elijah's" mission is to call God's people back to His Word. In this manner we truly are "declaring the Word of the LORD." If, in the spirit of Elijah, we call the people to "remember the Torah of Moses," then "righteousness is being restored."

Why remember Moses? Because we live in the end and have forgotten him, or more importantly, what he taught. When people enter a building they typically notice the furnishings, the walls, ceiling etc. Seldom do they take note of the fact that concealed beneath their feet is the foundation. Likewise, we in the end time have forgotten that what Moses taught is the foundation of our faith. When someone bites into an apple they enjoy the fruit, not the seed. Rarely do they stop to consider the seed except to toss it away. Even so, the seeds they toss away are the very reason and purpose for the apple's existence. The Torah, the Good Seed, is the life and essence of the Fruit.

Why should we remember Moses? Because Elijah, who comes at the end of days, is to be the forerunner of the coming Messianic era. Elijah is the one who "prepares the way of the LORD" and who "restores all things." This means that "Elijah" - you and I - must study and know the Torah because to study Moses is to study the Messiah. To know the Torah is to know Y'shua. To understand Moses is to understand the beginning and, consequently, to perceive the end of days.

"Phillip found Nathanael and said to him, 'We have found Him of whom Moses in the law, and also the prophets, wrote - Y'shua of Nazareth, the son of Joseph.' " - John 1:45

"Do not think that I shall accuse you to the Father; there is one who accuses you - Moses, in whom you trust. For if you believed Moses, you would believe Me; for he wrote about Me. but if you do not believe his writings, how will you believe My words?"
- John 5:45-47

"I am the Alef (alpha) and the Tav (omega), the Beginning and End, the First and the Last."
- Revelation 22:13

In Conclusion

"Surely the LORD God does nothing, unless He reveals His secret to His servants the prophets."
- Amos 3:7

On many occasions I have asked congregations if they were excited about what God was doing. They always answer with an enthusiastic "Amen!" Then I ask them "What is God doing?" I get the same answer everywhere - dead silence. The vast majority of God's people do not know in spite of the fact that God does reveal His secret *when it is time* for them to be revealed. If He reveals His secrets then, obviously, He wants His people to know His purpose and not be left in the dark. So, if some of the information I have shared has been somewhat new to you, *maybe* it is because *now* is the time for it to be revealed.

So then, being faced with a wealth of compelling evidence such as this, are we to continue ignoring the obvious for the sake of long-held eschatological traditions, treating them as if they were some kind of theological security blanket? Can we afford to continue interpreting the end from the end instead of, as we are directed, interpreting the end from the beginning? Are we courageous enough to reconsider some aspects of our theology?

Perhaps before now, some things we have shared would not have seemed so obvious. If what has been detailed in this book is true, then it means it is time for you to hear it. The Father wants His people to be informed and prepared for - not scared of - what is coming. You see, as partakers of the "covenants of promise" and as members of the "commonwealth of Israel" (Eph. 2:12), we have a significant role to play. We are to overcome the serpent. He should be beneath our heel. Remember, the sun-clothed woman - she who gives birth to the Promised Seed - stood with the *moon under her feet!*

That being said, we are not the Head, but the Body. The focus of history is not fixed upon you or me, but upon Him, for the testimony of Y'shua *is* the spirit of prophecy. To comprehend this is to understand He truly is *the beginning and the end*. Who and what we are and what we accomplish rests solely upon Him, the Author and Finisher of our faith. He is our Rock and sure Foundation. He is the Good Seed and soon He will crush the head of the serpent for all time, putting an end to the ancient enmity, and initiating a kingdom of joy, peace and justice. The end then, is merely the beginning of a new day!

SELECT BIBLIOGRAPHY

Al-Masih, Abd, *Who Is Allah In Islam?*. Villach, Austria: Light of Life Publishing.

Bader, Gershom, *The Encyclopedia of Talmudic Sages*. Northvale: Jason Aronson, 1988.

Delitzach, Franz & Keil, Johann, *Keil & Delitzsch Commentary on the Old Testament*.

Fregosi, Paul, *Jihad In The West*. Amherst: Prometheus Books, 1998.

Ginsburgh, Yitzchak, *The Alef-Beit*. Northvale: Jason Aronson, 1991.

Flavius, Josephus, *Antiquities of the Jews*. Grand Rapids: Kregel Publications, 1960.

Hourani, Albert, *A History of the Arab Peoples*. Cambridge: The Belknap Press, 1991.

Lancaster, D. Thomas, *Mystery of the Gospel: Jew and Gentile and the Eternal Purpose of God*. Littleton: First Fruits of Zion, 2003.

Metzger, Bruce & Coogan, Michael, *The Oxford Companion to the Bible*. New York: Oxford University Press, 1993.

Scharfstein, Zevi, *New Comprehensive Shilo Hebrew Dictionary*. New York: Shilo Publishing, 1973.

Stern, David H., *Jewish New Testament Commentary*, Clarksville: JNT Publications, 1992.

Schochet, Jacob Immanuel, *Mashiach*. Brooklyn: S.I.E., 1992.

Trifkovic, Serge, *The Sword of the Prophet: Islam History, Theology, Impact on the World*. Boston: Regina Orthodox Press, 2002.

Unterman, Alan, *Dictionary of Jewish Lore and Legend*. London: Thames and Hudson, 1991.

Vine, W.E., *Vine's Expository Dictionary of New Testament Words*. Iowa Falls: World Wide Publishers, 1981.

The Book of Daniel: Artscroll Tanach Series. Brooklyn: Mesorah Publications, 1979.

The Soncino Talmud. Brooklyn: Judaica Press.

The Soncino Pentateuch and Haftarahs. London: Soncino Press, 1973.

The Stone Edition Chumash. Brooklyn: Mesorah Publications, 2001.